Collins
gem

Collins Arabic phrasebook

Consultant

S.Abdi-Goulid

First published 2007

Reprint 10 9 8 7 6 5 4 3 2 1

Typeset by Davidson Pre-Press, Glasgow

Printed in Malaysia by Imago

www.collinslanguage.com

ISBN 13 978-000-724676-2

ISBN 10 0-00-724676-5

Using your phrasebook

Your *Collins Gem Phrasebook* is designed to help you locate the exact phrase you need, when you need it, whether on holiday or for business. If you want to adapt the phrases, you can easily see where to substitute your own words using the dictionary section, and the clear, full-colour layout gives you direct access to the different topics.

The Gem Phrasebook includes:

- Over 70 topics arranged thematically. Each phrase is accompanied by a simple pronunciation guide which eliminates any problems pronouncing foreign words.

- A top ten tips section to safeguard against any cultural faux pas, giving essential dos and don'ts for situations involving local customs or etiquette.

- Practical hints to make your stay trouble free, showing you where to go and what to do when dealing with everyday matters such as travel or hotels and offering valuable tourist information.

- Face to face sections so that you understand what is being said to you. These example mini-dialogues give you a good idea of what to expect from a real conversation.

- Common announcements and messages you may hear, ensuring that you never miss the important information you need to know when out and about.
- A clearly laid-out dictionary means you will never be stuck for words.
- A basic grammar section which will enable you to build on your phrases.
- A list of public holidays to avoid being caught out by unexpected opening and closing hours, and to make sure you don't miss the celebrations!

It's worth spending time before you embark on your travels just looking through the topics to see what is covered and becoming familiar with what might be said to you.

Whatever the situation, your *Gem Phrasebook* is sure to help!

Contents

Pronouncing Arabic

The Arabic alphabet is written and read from right to left and horizontally. There are 28 letters in the Arabic alphabet:

Name of letter	Arabic Letter	Name of letter	Arabic Letter
Taa (t)	ط	alif (ă)	أ
Thaa (th)	ظ	Baa (b)	ب
'ein (')	ع	Taa (t)	ت
Qain (q)	غ	Thaa (th)	ث
Faa (f)	ف	Jeem (j)	ج
Qaaf (q)	ق	Haa (h)	ح
Kaaf (k)	ك	Khaa (kh)	خ
Laam (l)	ل	Daal (da)	د
Miim (m)	م	Thaal (th)	ذ
Nuun (n)	ن	Raa (r)	ر
Haa (h)	هـ	Zaa (z)	ز
Waaw (w)	و	Seen (s)	س
Yaa (y)	ي	Sheen (sh)	ش
		Saad (s)	ص
		dhaad (dh)	ض

Pronouncing Arabic

The table below shows the letters that are similar to those in English, and that you should therefore have no problem learning or pronouncing.

Name of letter	Arabic letter	Sounds like
Alif (ă)	ا	apple
Baa (b)	ب	ball
Taa (t)	ت	ticket
Thaa (th)	ث	thick
Jeem (j)	ج	jam
Daal (da)	د	done
Thaal (th)	ذ	though
Raa (r)	ر	rat
Zaa (z)	ز	zoo
Seen (s)	س	sad
Sheen (sh)	ش	shop

Name of letter	Arabic letter	Sounds like
Saad (s)	ص	sorry
Taa (t)	ط	tip
Thaa (th)	ظ	thaw
Faa (f)	ف	far
Kaaf (k)	ك	cat
Laam (l)	ل	lot
Miim (m)	م	mother
Nuun (n)	ن	nun
Haa (h)	هـ	hand
Waaw (w)	و	wood
Yaa (y)	ي	yes

Unfamiliar sounds

The Arabic letters below are the ones that are either hard to pronounce or are pronounced a little bit differently.

Name of letter	Arabic letter	Sounds like
Haa (h)	ح	Similar to **h** in house
Khaa (kh)	خ	Similar to **ch** in loch
'ein (')	ع	Similar to **a** in another
Ghain (q)	غ	Similar to a French **r** sound
Qaaf (q)	ق	Like **q** but a little bit sharper

Top ten tips

There are some social conventions and local customs that visitors should be aware of when travelling in Arab countries. Many traditional customs and beliefs are tied up with religion, and Islam (the main religion in most Arab countries) has a clear influence on how people live and behave.

1 A handshake is the customary form of greeting.

2 Many of the manners and social customs are similar to French manners, particularly amongst the middle classes.

3 Visitors may find, in some social situations, that being patient and firm pays dividends.

4 Often, visitors may find themselves the centre of unsolicited attention. In towns, young boys after money will be eager to point out directions, sell goods or simply charge for a photograph, while unofficial guides will offer advice or services. Visitors should be courteous, but wary of the latter.

5 Women travelling alone, and/or wearing clothes regarded as procovative (e.g. revealing tops, short skirts, etc.) may attract unwanted attention.

6 Sexual relations outside marriage, and homosexual conduct are punishable by law.

7 Smoking is widespread and it is customary to offer cigarettes. In most cases it is obvious where not to smoke, except during Ramadan when it is illegal to eat, drink or smoke in public.

8 Dress should be conservative and women should not wear revealing clothes, particularly when in religious buildings and in towns. Western style clothing is, however, accepted in modern nightclubs, restaurants, hotels and bars in tourist destinations.

9 In Egypt tourists have to pay a fee to take photographs inside pyramids, tombs and museums.

10 Alcohol is tolerated, with non-Muslims allowed to drink alcohol in the city bars, restaurants, clubs and hotels.

Talking to people

Hello/goodbye, yes/no

Body language is very important when dealing with Arabs. You will see that when they talk, they often use their hands to describe what they are saying.

Please	من فضلك min fadlak
Thank you	شكرا لك shuk-ran laka
Thanks	شكرا shuk-ran
Yes	نعم na-'am

No	لا la
Sorry!	آسف! aa-sif
Excuse me!	لو سمحت! law sa-mah-t!
Hello/Hi	مرحبا/سلام mar-ha-ba/salaam
Goodbye	الى اللقاء/مع السلامة ilal-li-qaa/ma-'as-sa-laa-ma
Good morning	صباح الخير sa-baa-hul-khayr
Good afternoon	مساء الخير ma-sa-ul-khayr
Good day	نهار سعيد na-haar sa-'iid
Good evening	مساء الخير ma-sa-ul-khayr

Goodnight	ليلة سعيدة lay-la-tun sa-'ii-da
I don't understand	لم أفهم lam af-ham
I don't speak Arabic	لا اتكلم العربية laa af-ha-mul-'a-ra-biy-ya

Key phrases

Is there...?/ Are there...?	هل هناك...؟ hal hu-naa-ka...?
Do you have...?	هل عندك...؟ hal 'in-da-ka...?
Do you have bread?	هل عندك خبز؟ hal 'in-da-ka khubz?
Do you have milk?	هل عندك حليب؟ hal 'in-da-ka halib?

Do you have stamps?	هل عندك طوابع بريد؟ hal 'in-da-ka ta-waa-bi' ba-rii-diy-ya?
I want/need...	أنا أريد... anaa u-rii-du...
I want a loaf	أنا أريد رغيفا anaa u-rii-du ra-ghifan
I want this	أنا أريد هذا anaa u-rii-du haa-thaa
I don't want this	لا أريد هذا laa u-rii-du haa-thaa
How much is this?	بكم هذا؟ bi-kem haa-thaa?
How many?	كم واحدة؟ kem waa-hi-da?
When is...?	متى...؟ ma-taa...?

When is breakfast?	متى وقت الفطور؟ ma-taa waq-tul fu-tuur?
What time is it?	كم الساعة؟ kem as-saa-'ah?
At what time...?	في أي ساعة...؟ fii ay-yi saa-'ah...?
Where is...?	أين...؟ ay-na...?
Where is the bank?	أين البنك؟ ay-nal bank?
Where is the toilet?	أين المرحاض؟ ay-nal mir-haad?
Which one?	أي واحد؟ ay-yu waa-hid?
Why?	لماذا؟ li-maa-thaa?
Please go away!	أتركني لو سمحت! ut-ruk-nii law sa-mah-t!

Is...included?	هل ... في الحساب؟ hal ... fil hi-saab?
a/an/one ... please	واحدة من فضلك ... ... waa-hida min fad-lak
two teas please	كأسين شاي من فضلك ka' sein shai min fad-lak
some ... please	قليل من ... من فضلك qa-liil min ... min fad-lak

Signs and notices

مفتوح	maf-tuuh	open
مغلق	muqlaq	closed
سيدات	say-yidaat	ladies
رجال	ri-jaal	gentlemen
خدمة ذاتية	khidma thaa-tiy-yah	self-service
ادفع	id-fa'	push
اسحب	is-hab	pull
المحاسب	al-mu-haasib	cash desk

ماء شرب	maa shurb	drinking water
مراحيض	maraa-hiid	toilets
شاغر	shaaqir	vacant
مشغول	mash-quul	engaged
جناح الطوارئ	janaahut-tawaari	emergency department
الإسعافات الأولية	al-is'aafaa-tul-aw-waliy-ya	first aid
ممتلئ	mumta-li	full
قف	qif	stop
معطل	mu'attal	out of order
للإيجار	lil-iijaar	for hire/rent
للبيع	lil-bay-'	for sale
تنزيلات	tan-ziilaat	sales
الطابق تحت الأرض	at-taabiq tahtal-ard	basement
الطابق الأرضي	at-taabiq al-ardii	ground floor
دخول	du-khuul	entrance
مكتب التذاكر	maktabut-tathaakir	ticket office
محطة الشرطة	mahata-tush-shur-tah	police station

الأشياء الضائعة	al-ash-yaa ad-daa-i-'ah	lost property
مغادرة/ إقلاع	muqadarah/ iqlaa'	departures
وصول	wusuul	arrivals
ممنوع	mamnuu'	prohibited
الحقائب المتركة	al-haqaa-ib al-matruukah	left luggage
خاص	khaas	private
ساخن	saakhin	hot
بارد	baarid	cold
خطر	khatar	danger
ممنوع التدخين	mam-nuu-'ut-tadkhiin	no smoking
لا تلمس	laa talmas	do not touch
خروج	khuruuj	exit
غرفة تغيير الملابس	qurfat taq-yiir al-malaabis	changing room
الحمام	al-ham-maam	bathroom
احذر!	ih-thar!	caution!
معلومات	ma'-luumaat	information
استعلامات	isti'-laamaat	enquiries

Polite expressions

As in every culture, good manners are very important to Arabs. You may experience excessive politeness when people meet each other. Hugging and kissing on both cheeks is very normal. People often kiss the hand of elderly people out of respect. To address someone formally, use **as-say-yid** for men or **as-say-yida** for women before their first name, for example, **As-say-yid Ahmed**; **As-say-yida Faatima**. This may vary from country to country.

There are several styles of greeting in use; it is best to wait for your counterpart to initiate the greeting. Men shake hands with other men. Some men will shake hands with women, however, it is advisable for businesswomen to wait for a man to offer his hand. A more traditional greeting between men involves grasping each other's right hand, placing the left hand on the other's right shoulder and exchanging kisses on each cheek.

How do you do? كيف حالك؟
kay-fa haa-luk?

Talking to people

Pleased to meet you	أنا سعيد لرؤيتك anaa sa-'ii-dun li ru-ya-ti-ka
Thank you	شكرا لك shuk-ran laka
I am fine	أنا بخير ana bi-khayr
Welcome!	أهلا و سهلا! ah-lan wa sah-lan!
Here you are	تفضل tafad-dal
Pardon?	عذراً 'uth-ran
This is...	...هذا.../ هذه haa-thaa ... (m)/haa-thihii (f)
This is my husband	هذا زوجي haa-thaa zaw-jii
This is my wife	هذه زوجتي haa-thi-hii zaw-jatii

Enjoy your meal! وجبة هنية!
waj-ba ha-niy-yah!

The meal was delicious كانت وجبتاً لذيذة
kaa-nat waj-batan la-thii-thah

Thank you very much شكراً جزيلاً لك
shuk-ran ja-ziilan lak

Have a good trip! رحلة سعيدة!
rih-la sa-'iidah!

Enjoy your holiday! عطلة ممتعة!
'ut-la-tun mum-ti'ah!

Celebrations

Happy birthday! عيد ميلاد سعيد!
'ied-mii-laad sa-'iid!

Congratulations! مبروك!
mab-ruuk!

Cheers!	هنيئا han-nii-an
Happy New Year!	عام جديد سعيد! 'aa-mun ja-dii-dun sa-'iid!

Making friends

What's your name?	ماسمك؟ mas-muk?
My name is...	اسمي... is-mii...
How old are you?	كم عمرك؟ kem 'um-ruka?
I'm ... years old	أنا ... سنة anaa ... sa-nah
Where do you live?	أين تسكن؟ ay-na tas-kun?

I live...	أنا أسكن ... anaa as-ku-nu...
in London	في لندن fii len-den
in Australia	في أستراليا fii australia
Where are you from?	من أين أنت؟ min ay-na anta?
I'm English	أنا إنجليزي ana inglezi
I'm Canadian	أنا كندي ana kanadi
Are you married?	هل أنت متزوج؟ hal anta mu-ta-zaw-wij?
Do you have children?	هل لديك أطفال؟ hal la-day-ka at-faal?
I have children	عندي أطفال 'in-dii at-faal

I don't have children	ليس عندي أطفال lay-sa 'in-dii at-faal
I have a boyfriend	عندي صديق 'in-dii sa-diiq
I have a girlfriend	عندي صديقة 'in-dii sa-dii-qah
I'm single	أنا عازب anaa 'a-zib
I'm married	أنا متزوج anaa mu-ta-zaw-wij
I'm divorced	أنا مطلق/مطلقة anaa mu-tal-liq (m) mu-tal-laqa (f)

Work

What is your job?	ما وظيفتك؟ maa wa-thii-fa-tuk?

> **Leisure/beach** (p 84) > **Sport** (p 90)

Do you enjoy it?	هل تستمتع بها؟ hal tas tam ti'u bi-ha?
I'm a doctor	أنا (طبيب) دكتور anaa ta-biib (dok-toor)
I'm a teacher	أنا معلم anaa mu-'al-lim
I'm a nurse	أنا ممرض anaa mu-mar-rid
I work in a shop	أنا أعمل في دكان anaa a'-ma-lu fii duk-kaan
I work in a factory	أنا أعمل في مصنع anaa a'-ma-lu fii mas-na'
I work in a bank	أنا أعمل في بنك anaa a'-ma-lu fii bank
I work from home	أنا أعمل من البيت anaa a'-ma-lu minal-bayt

Weather

مشرق mush-riq	clear
ممطر mum-tir	rainy
بارد baa-rid	cold
حار haa-r	hot
مُشمس mush-mis	sunny

It's sunny — يوم مشمس
yaw-mun mush-mis

It's raining — يوم ممطر
yaw-mun mum-tir

It's windy — يوم عاصف
yaw-mun 'aa-sif

It's very hot — يوم حار جداً
yaw-mun haar jid-dan

What is the temperature? — ما هي درجة الحرارة؟
maa hiya dara-ja-tul ha-raa-rah?

What is the weather forecast for tomorrow?	ما هي النشرة الجوية غداً؟ maa hiya an-nash-ra-tul-jaw-wiy-ya-tu qa-dan?
Does it get cool at night?	هل تصبح باردة في الليل؟ hal tus-bi-hu baa-ri-dah fil-lay-l?
Will there be a storm?	هل ستكون هناك عاصفة؟ hal sa-ta-kuu-nu hu-naa-ka 'aa-sifa?
What beautiful weather!	ما أجمل الطقس! maa aj-ma-lat-taq-s!
What awful weather!	ما اسوء الطقس! maa as-wa-at-taqs!

Getting around

Asking the way

يسار ya-saa-r	left
يمين ya-miin	right
على طول 'alaa tuul	straight on
قريب من qa-riib min	next to
مقابل mu-qaa-bil	opposite
إشارة مرور ishaa-ra-tu mu-ruur	traffic lights
عند المنعطف 'in-dal mun-'ataf	at the corner

FACE TO FACE

A لو سمحت، أين مكتب البريد؟
law sa-mah-ta, ay-na mak-ta-bul-ba-riid
Excuse me! Where is the post office?

B استمر إلى الأمام ثم انعطف إلى اليمين عند المنعطف
is-tamir ilal-amaam thum-ma in-atif ilal-yamiin 'in-dal mun-'ataf
Keep straight on and turn right at the corner

A هل هو بعيد؟
hal hu-wa ba-'iid
Is it far?

B ٢ دقائق فقط
da-qii-qa-taan fa-qat
Two minutes away

A شكراً لك
shuk-ran laka
Thank you

B على الرحب و السعة
'a-lar-rahb was-sa'ah
You are welcome

Where is...?	أين... ay-na...
Where is the museum?	أين المتحف؟ ay-nal mit-haf?

How do I get...?	كيف أصل إلى....؟ key-fa asi-lu ilaa...?
How do I get to the museum?	كيف أصل إلى المتحف؟ key-fa asi-lu ila-l mit-haf?
to the coach station	إلى محطة الباص ilaa ma-hat-tat al-baas
to the beach	إلى الشاطئ ila-sh-shaa-ti
to my hotel	إلى فندقي ilaa fun-du-qii
Is it far?	هل هو بعيد؟ hal hu-wa ba-'iid?

YOU MAY HEAR...	
انحنِ/لفْ يسار in-hani/lif ya-saar	Turn left
انحنِ/لفْ يمين in-hani/lif ya-miin	Turn right
استمر إلى الأمام is-ta-mir ila-l amaam	Keep straight on

Bus and coach

In some Arab countries, if you are male, you will have to take a seat at the rear of the bus and leave the front seats for the female passengers.

باص أو حافلة baas/hafila	coach/bus
موقف الباص maw-qif al-baas	bus stop
محطة الباصات ma-hat-tat al-baa-saat	coach station
تذكرة that-karah	ticket

FACE TO FACE

A لو سمحت. أين الباص المقلع في الساعة السابعة صباحاً إلى القاهرة؟
law sa-mah-t. Ay-nal-baas al-muq-li' fis-saa'atis-saabi-'ah sa-baa-han ilaa Al-qaa-hi-ra?
Excuse me. Which one is the 7 o'clock bus to Cairo?

B الباص على اليمين. الباص الأزرق
al-baas 'a-laal-ya-miin. al-baas al-az-raq
The one on the right. The blue bus.

A شكرا
shukran
Thanks

Where is the coach station?	أين محطة الباصات؟ ay-na ma-hat-tat al-baa-saat?
I am going to...	أنا ذاهب إلى... anaa thaa-hi-bun ilaa...
Is there a bus to...?	هل هناك باص إلى... hal hu-naa-ka baas-sun ilaa...
Does it go to...?	هل يذهب إلى... hal yath-ha-bu ilaa...
to the airport	إلى المطار ilal-mataar
to the beach	إلى الشاطئ ilash-shaati
to the centre	إلى مركز المدينة ilaa mar-kaz al-ma-dii-nah
one ticket	تذكرة واحدة tath-ka-ra-tun waa-hida
two tickets	تذكرتان tath-ka-ra-taan

three tickets	٣ تذاكر tha-laa-thu ta-thaa-kir
When is the next bus?	متى يصل الباص التالي؟ ma-taa ya-si-lul baa-sut-taa-lii?

YOU MAY HEAR...	
لا يوجد باص laa yuu-ja-du baas	There is no bus
يجب أن تأخذ سيارة أجرة ya-ji-b an ta-khu-tha say-yaa-ra-ta uj-ra	You must take a taxi

Metro

Cairo has got a metro system.

مدخل mad-khal	entrance
مخرج makh-raj	way out

> **Luggage** (p 111)

Where is the nearest metro station?	أين أقرب محطة مترو (أنفاق)؟ ay-na aq-rab ma-hat-tat metro (an-faaq)?
How does the ticket machine work?	كيف تُستخدَم آلة التذاكر؟ kay-fa tus-takh-dam aa-lat at-ta-thaa-kir?
Do you have a map of the metro?	هل لديك خريطة للمترو؟ hal la-day-ka kha-rii-ta lil metro?
I'm going to...	أنا ذاهب إلى... anaa thaa-hib ilaa...
How do I/we get to...?	كيف أصل إلى... kay-fa a-si-lu ilaa...
Do I have to change?	هل يجب علي أن أغير الحافلة؟ hal ya-ji-bu 'a-lay-ya an u-qay-yira al-haafila?
What is the next stop?	ما هو الموقف التالي؟ maa hu-wa al-maw qif at-taa-lii?

Excuse me! I'm getting off here	لو سمحت! أنا نازل هنا law sa-mah-t! anaa naa-zil hunaa
Please let me through	لو سمحت، دعني أمر law sa-mah-t, da'-nii amur

Train

محطة ma-hat-ta	station
قطار qi-taar	train
منصة mi-nas-sa	platform
مقعد maq-'ad	seat
تذكرة that-ka-ra	ticket
مكتب الحجز mak-tab al-haj-z	booking office
جدول مواعيد jad-wal ma-waa-'iid	timetable
وصلة was-lah	connection

FACE TO FACE

A متى موعد القطار التالي إلى إزمر؟
ma-taa maw-'id al-qi-taar at-taa-lii ilaa Monastir?
When is the next train to Monastir?

B في الساعة السابعة
fis-saa-'a-tis saa-bi-'a
At 7 o'clock

A ثلاثة تذاكر من فضلك
tha-laa-tha-tu ta-thaa-kir min fad-lak
Three tickets please

B ذهاب (فقط) أم ذهاب و إياب؟
tha-haab (fa-qat) am tha-haab wa i-yaab?
Single or return?

A ذهاب و إياب، من فضلك
tha-haab wa i-yaab min fad-lak
Return please

Where is the station?	أين المحطة؟ ay-nal ma-hat-ta?
a single	تذكرة واحدة ذهاب فقط tath-ka-ra waa-hi-da tha-haab fa-qat

two singles	تذكرتان ذهاب فقط that-ka-ra-taan tha-haab fa-qat
a single to Monastir	تذكرة ذهاب فقط إلى ازمير that-ka-rat tha-haab fa-qat ilaa Monastir
two singles to Alexandria	تذكرتان ذهاب فقط إلى الاسكندرية that-ka-ra-taan tha-haab fa-qat ilaa Alexandria
a return	تذكرة واحدة ذهاب و إياب that-ka-ra waa-hida tha-haab wa i-yaab
two returns	تذكرتان ذهاب و إياب that-ka-ra-taan tha-haab wa i-yaab
one adult	بالغ واحد baa-liq waa-hid
two children	طفلان tif-laan

two adults	بالغان baa-li-qaan
first class	درجة اولى da-ra-jah uu-laa
second class	درجة ثانية da-ra-jah thaa-ni-yah
smoking	المدخنين qayr al-mu-da-khi-niin
non-smoking	غير المدخنين al-mu-da-khi-niin
I want to book a seat	أريد أن أحجز مقعدا u-rii-du an ah-jiza maq-‘adan
Which platform?	أيّ رصيف؟ ay-yu ra-siif?
When does it get to Cairo?	متى سيصل القاهرة؟ ma-taa sa-ya-si-lu Al Qahira?
When does it leave?	متى يغادر؟ ma-taa yu-qaa-dir?

When does it arrive? | متى يصل؟
ma-taa ya-sil?

Is this seat free? | هل هذا المقعد شاغر؟
hal haa-thal-maq-'ad shaa-qir?

Excuse me! | آسف!
aa-sif!

Occupied | مأخوذ
ma-khuu-th

Taxi

There are plenty of taxis in cities, towns and resorts. It is always wise to check the price before a long journey. Taxis can be shared, which is a cheaper option, but you will have to wait until all the seats are occupied. Taxi in Arabic is also '**taxi**', but you might also hear '**uj-rah**' which literally means 'hire'. '**Taxi**' is used throughout the following section. Alternatively, there are minibuses which provide transport over short distances.

> **Luggage** (p 111)

Where can I get a taxi?	أين أجد تاكسي؟ ay-na a-ji-du taksi?
I want to go to...	أريد الذهاب إلى... u-rii-du ath-tha-haa-ba ilaa...
How much is it?	كم قيمتها؟ kam qii-ma-tu-haa?
To the airport, please	إلى المطار من فضلك ilal-ma-taar min fad-lak
To the beach, please	إلى الشاطئ من فضلك ilash-shaa-ti min fad-lak
Please stop here	قف هنا لو سمحت qif-hunaa law sa-mah-t
Please wait	انتظر لو سمحت in-ta-thir law sa-mah-t
It's too expensive	هذا غالي جداً haa-thaa qaa-li jid-dan
I've no change	ليس عندي صرف lay-saa 'in-dii sarf
Keep the change	خذ الباقي khuth al-baa-qii

Boat and ferry

Boats and ferries are not considered a main mode of transport in most of the Arab world. Occasionally small boats are used to cross canals and rivers in some countries such as Egypt. This is due to the fact that most Arab countries do not have canal or river systems.

مكتب التذاكر mak-tab at-ta-thaa-kir	ticket office
تذكرة للعبّارة that-ka-ra lil-'ab-baa-rah	token for ferry
جدول المواعيد jad-wal al-ma-waa-'iid	timetable
الوصول al-wu-suul	arrival
المغادرة al-mu-qaa-da-ra	departure
القارب المزعنف al-qaa-rib al-mu-za'-naf	hydrofoil

one token	تذكرة واحدة tath-ka-ra waa-hi-da
two tokens	تذكرتان that-ka-ra-taan
three tokens	ثلاث تذاكر tha-laa-thu ta-thaa-kir
When is the next boat?	متى المركب القادم؟ ma-tal mar-ka-bul qaa-dim?
When is the last boat?	متى المركب الأخير؟ ma-tal mar-ka-bul a-khii-r?
Is there a hydrofoil?	هَلْ هناك قارب مزعنف؟ hal hu-naa-ka qaa-rib mu-za'-naf?
We want to go to...	نُريدُ الذهاب إلى... nu-rii-duth-tha-haa-ba ila...
Is there a timetable?	هَلْ هناك جدول مواعيد؟ hal hu-naa-ka jad-wal ma-waa-'iid?

When does the boat leave? | متى يرحل المركب؟
ma-taa yar-ha-lu al-mar-kab?

How long does it take? | كَمْ مِنَ الوقت يأخذ؟
kam min al-waq-ti ya-khu-th?

Air travel

المطار	al-ma-taar	airport
البوابة	al-baw-waa-ba	gate
القادمون	al-qaa-di-muun	arrivals
المغادرة	al-mu-qaa-da-rah	departures
الطيران	at-ta-ya-raan	flight
محلي	ma-hal-li	domestic
دولي	du-wa-li	international
المعلومات	al-ma'-luu-maat	information

To the airport, please | إلى المطارِ، رجاءً
ilal ma-taar, ra-jaa-an

My flight is at ... o'clock | طيارتي في الساعة ...
tay-yaa-ra-tii fis-saa-'a ...

How much is it to the airport?	كَمْ التسعيرة إلى المطارِ؟ kam at-tas-'ii-rah ilal ma-taar?
How much is it to the town centre?	كَمْ التسعيرة إلى مركزِ البلدة؟ kam at-tas-'ii-rah ilaa mar-kaz al ma-dii-na?
When will the flight leave?	متى تقلع الطائرة؟ ma-taa tuq-li-'ut-taa-ira?

YOU MAY HEAR...

إذهبْ إلى البوابة رقم... ith-hab ilal-baw-waa-bah ra-qam...	Go to gate number...

> **Luggage** (p 111)

Customs control

The import, export, possession and use of drugs is strictly forbidden and penalties for offenders are extremely severe.

جواز السفر ja-waa-z as-sa-far	passport
جمارك ja-maa-rik	customs
خمر/كحول khamr/ku-huul	alcohol
دخان dukh-khaan (you may also hear: تبغ = tabq)	tobacco

Do I have to pay duty on this? هَلْ عليَّ أنْ أدْفعَ ضريبةَ على هذه؟
hal 'a-lay-ya an ad-fa'a da-rii-bah 'a-laa haa-thaa?

It is my medicine إنه دوائي
in-na-huu da-waa-ii

I bought this duty-free إشتريتُ هذا غير خاضع للضريبة
ish-ta-ray-tu haa-thaa al-qayr khaa-di' lid-da-rii-bah

Driving

Car hire

مفاتيح ma-faa-tiih	keys
وثائق التأمين wa-thaa-iq at-ta-miin	insurance documents
رخصة القيادة rukh-satul-qi-yaa-dah	driving licence

I want to hire a car — أُريدُ إسْتئجار سيارة
u-rii-du is-ti-gaar say-yaarah

with automatic gears — بالجير (تروس) الآلية
bil-gear (tu-ruus) al-aali

for one day — ليوم واحد
li yawm waa-hid

for two days — ليومين
li yaw-mayn

How much is it?	كم قيمتها؟ kam qii-ma-tu-haa?
Is insurance included?	هل هذا يتضمن التأمين؟ hal haa-thaa ya-ta-dam-man at-ta-miin?
Is there a deposit to pay?	هل هناك ايداع للدفع؟ hal hu-naa-ka ii-daa' lid-daf'?
Can I pay by credit card?	هل من الممكن أن أدفع بالبطاقة الائتمانية؟ hal mi-nal mum-kin an ad-fa'a bil-bi-taa-qah al-i-ti-maa-ni-yah?
What petrol does it take?	ما نوع الوقود؟ maa naw-'ul wa-quud?

Driving and petrol

انتبه/خطر in-ta-bih/kha-tar	caution/danger
قف qif	stop
خط سريع khat sa-rii'	motorway
مركز المدينة mar-kaz al-ma-dii-nah	town centre

Can I park here? هل مسموح أن أقف هنا؟
hal mas-muu-h an a-qi-fa huna?

How long can I park for? إلى متى ممكن أقف هنا؟
ila ma-taa mum-kin a-qif hunaa?

We are driving to... نحن ذاهبون إلى...
nah-nu thaa-hi-buu-na ila...

Is the road good? هل الشارع جيد؟
halish-shaa-ri-'u jay-yid?

How long will it take? كم ستستغرق الرحلة؟
kam sa-tas-taq-riq ar-rih-la?

YOU MAY HEAR...	
أنت تسير بسرعة عالية جداً an-ta ta-sii-ru bi sur-'a 'aa-li-yah jid-dan	You are driving too fast
رخصة قيادتك رجاء rukh-sa-tu qi-yaa-da-ti-ka ra-jaa-an	Your driving licence please

Petrol is widely available on main roads.

بترول bat-rool	petrol
البنزين الخالي من الرّصاص al-ban-ziin al-khaa-li min ar-ra-saas	unleaded petrol
ديزل dii-zal	diesel

Where is the nearest petrol station? — أين أقرب محطة البنزين؟ ay-na aq-ra-bu ma-hat-ta-tul bin-ziin?

Fill it up, please — إملأه، رجاء im-la-hu, ra-jaa-an

Please check the oil — رجاء افحص الزيت ra-jaa-an, if-has az-zay-t

Can I pay by credit card?

هل من الممكن أن أدفع ببطاقة الائتمان؟

hal mi-nal mum-kin an ad-fa'a bi-bi-taa-qah al-i-ti-maa-n?

YOU MAY HEAR...	
ليس لدينا... lay-sa la-day-naa...	We have no...
أنت تحتاج إلى زيت an-ta tah-taa-ju ilaa zayt	You need oil
أنت تحتاج إلى ماء an-ta tah-taa-ju ilaa maa	You need water
أنت تحتاج إلى هواء an-ta tah-taa-ju ilaa ha-waa	You need air

Breakdown

If you break down on the motorway, go to the nearest service station and ask for help. It is normal to ask other road users for help and they are usually more than happy to assist.

My car has broken down	تعطلت سيارتي	ta-'at-ta-lat say-yaa-ra-tii
Can you help me?	هل تستطيع أن تساعدني؟	hal-tas-ta-tii-'u an tu-saa-'i-da-nii?
I've run out of petrol	انتهى البترول عندي	in-ta-hal bat-roo-lu 'in-dii
I have a flat tyre	عندي إطار فارغ	'in-dii i-taar faa-riq
Where is the nearest garage? (repair shop)	أين أقرب ورشة لتصليح السيارات؟	ay-na aq-rab war-sha li-tas-liih as-say-yaa-raat?
Can you repair it?	هل يمكنك تصليحها؟	hal-yum-ki-nu-ka tas-lii-hu-haa?
How long will it take?	كم من الوقت ستأخذ؟	kam minal waq-ti sa-ta-khu-th?
How much will it cost?	كم ستكلف من المال؟	kam sa-tu-kal-lif minal maal?

Breakdown

Car parts

Local garages are able to repair cars very quickly. Repairs are carried out in industrial zones called si-naa-'iy-yah, which are located in the industrial estates of towns.

...doesn't work	لا تعمل ... ... laa ta'-mal	
Where is the repair shop?	أين ورشة التصليح؟ ay-na war-shat at-tas-liih?	
accelerator	المعجّل	al-mu-'aj-jil
alternator	المولد الكهربائي	al-mu-wal-lid al-kah-ru-baa-I
battery	البطارية	al-bat-taa-riya
brakes	الكابحات	al-kaa-bi-haat
choke	الشراقة	ash-shar-raa-qa
clutch	الفاصِل	al-faa-sil
engine	المحرّك	al-mu-har-rik
exhaust pipe	أنبوب العادم	un-buub al-'aa-dim
fuse	المصهر	al-mis-har
gears	التروس	at-tu-ruus

handbrake	كابح يدوي	kaa-bih ya-da-wi
headlights	الأضواء العلوية	al-ad-waa al-'ul-wiy-yah
ignition	الإيقاد	al-ii-qaad
ignition key	مفتاح الإشتعال	mif-taah al-ish-ti-'aal
indicator	المؤشر	al-mu-ash-shir
lock	القفل	al-qifl
radiator	راديا تور/مبرد المحرك	raad-yaa-tor/ mu-ba-rid al-mu-har-rik
reverse gear	الترس العكسي	at-turs al-'ak-si
seat belt	حزام المقعد	hi-zaam al-miq-'ad
spark plug	شمعة القدح	sham-'atul-qad-h
steering wheel	دولاب القيادة	duu-laab al-qi-yaa-da
tyre	الإطار	al-i-taar
wheel	العجلة	al-'a-ja-la
windscreen	الزجاجة الأمامية	az-zu-jaa-ja al-amaa-miy-ya
windscreen wiper	ماسحة الزجاجة الأمامية	maa-si-hat az-zu-jaa-ja al-amaa-miy-ya

Car parts

Staying somewhere

Hotel (booking)

Hotels are rated from 1 to 5 stars, although unstarred hotels also exist. In tourist areas it is easy to find a hotel or guesthouse. Breakfast will probably not be included in the room price.

We would like to book a single room	نودّ أن نحجز غرفة لشخص na-wad-du an nah-ji-za qur-fa li-shakhs
We would like to book a double room	نودّ أن نحجز غرفة لشخصين na-wad-du an nah-ji-za qur-fa li-shakh-sayn
For how many nights?	لكم ليلة؟ li-kam lay-lah?

for one night	لليلة واحدة li-lay-lah waa-hi-da
two nights	ليلتين li-lay-la-tayn
one week	لأسبوع li-us-buu'
Is there a hotel nearby?	هل هناك فندق قريب؟ hal hu-naa-ka fun-duq qa-riib?
Is there a guesthouse nearby?	هل هناك بيت للضيوف قريب؟ hal hu-naa-ka bayt lit-tu-yuuf qa-riib?
Do you have a room?	هل لديك غرفة؟ hal la-day-ka qur-fa?
I'd like...	أريد... u-rii-du...
a single room	غرفة لشخص qur-fa li-sha-kh-s
a double room	غرفة لشخصين qur-fa li sha-kh-sayn

a room for three people	غرفة لـ ٣ أشخاص qur-fa li 3 (tha-laatha) ash-khaas
with shower	بِدُش bi-dush
with bath	بحوض الإغتسال bi-haw-d al-iq-ti-saal
How much is it per night?	كم قيمتها في الليلة؟ kam qii-ma-tu-haa fil-lay-lah?
Is breakfast included?	هل هذا يتضمن الفطور؟ hal haa-thaa ya-ta-tham-ma-nu al-if-taar?
I'll be staying...	سأمكث... sa-am-ku-thu...
We'll be staying...	سنمكث... sa-nam-ku-thu...
one night	ليلة واحده lay-la waa-hi-da

two nights — ليلتان
lay-la-taan

three nights — ثلاث ليالي
tha-laa-thu la-yaa-lii

Is there anywhere else to stay? — هل هناك أي مكان آخر يمكن المكوث فيه؟
hal-hu-naa-ka ay-yu ma-kaa-nin aa-khar yum-ki-nul mu-kuu-tha fiih?

YOU MAY HEAR...	
اسمك، لو سمحت is-muka law sa-mah-t	Your name, please
جواز السفر، لو سمحت ja-waa-zus-sa-far law sa-mah-t	Your passport, please
المكان ممتلئ al-ma-kaan mum-ta-li	We are full

Hotel desk

I have a reservation	عندي حجز 'in-dii haj-z
My name is...	اسمي... is-mii...
Have you a different room?	هل لديك غرفة مختلفة؟ hal la-day-ka qur-fa mukh-ta-li-fa?
Where can I park the car?	أين يمكن أن أوقف السيارة؟ ay-na yum-ki-nu an uu-qi-fas-say-yaa-rah?
What time is breakfast?	ما وقت الفطور؟ maa waq-tul-fu-tuur?
What time is dinner?	ما وقت العشاء؟ maa waq-tul-'a-shaa?
The key, please	المفتاح، لو سمحت al-mif-taah law sa-mah-t

Room number...	غرفة رقم... qur-fa ra-qam...
Are there any messages for me?	هل هناك أي رسائل لي؟ hal hu-naa-ka ay-yu ra-saa-il lii?
I'm leaving tomorrow	أنا مغادر غدا anaa mu-qaa-dir qa-dan
Please prepare the bill	حضّر الفاتورة من فضلك had-dir al-faa-tuu-rah min fad-lak

Camping

Due to the weather, camping is not a particularly popular activity. There are no camp sites like the ones that can be found in the West. You might, however, find yourself camping in the desert of one of the gulf countries for couple of days. It is unlikely that you will see the word 'showers' anywhere. The word 'toilets' '**ham-maa-maat**' is sufficient.

مخيم mu-khay-yam	camp site
ماء للشرب maa lish-shurb	drinking water
الأدشاش al-ad-shaa-sh	showers
مكتب mak-tab	office
الإستقبال al-is-tiq-baal	reception
خيمة	tent

Where is the camp site? — أين المخيم؟
ay-nal mu-khay-yam?

How much is it per night? — كم سعره باللّيلة؟
kam si'-ru-hu bil-lay-la?

We want to stay... — نود أن نبقى...
na-wad-du an nab-qaa...

one night — ليلة واحده
lay-latun waa-hi-da

two nights — ليلتان
lay-la-taan

one week — أسبوع واحد
us-buu-'un waa-hid

Where is/are the...?	أين الـ...؟ ay-na al...?
toilets	حمامات ham-maa-maat
showers	الأدشاش al-ad-shaa-sh
drinking water	ماء للشرب maa lish-shurb

YOU MAY HEAR...	
المكان ممتلئ al-ma-kaan mum-ta-li	We are full

Self-catering

Can you give us an extra set of keys?	هل يمكن أن تعطينا مجموعة إضافيّة من المفاتيح؟ hal yum-kin an tu'-ti-naa maj-muu-'a i-thaa-fiy-ya min al-ma-faa-tiih?

Who do we contact if there are problems?	من نتّصل به إذا كان هناك مشاكل؟ man nat-ta-si-lu bi-hi i-thaa kaa-na hu-naa-ka ma-shaa-kil?
Is there always hot water?	هل هناك ماء ساخن دائماً؟ hal-hu-naa-ka maa-un saa-khin?
Where is the nearest supermarket?	أين أقرب سوبر ماركت؟ ay-na aq-ra-bu su-per-mar-kit?
Where do we leave the rubbish?	أين نترك القمامة؟ ay-na nat-ru-kul qu-maa-mah?

> **Sightseeing and tourist office** (p 81)

Shopping

Shopping phrases

Shops are generally open from 9 am to well after midnight, seven days a week. Some shops close between 12 and 4 pm due to the warm weather, and for siestas. You may also find some shops are closed at prayer times for about 10 minutes. Most towns have a farmers' market **bazar** once a week. At these, good-natured haggling and bargaining is normal: offer half to two-thirds of the asking price, then settle on a price somewhere in between. If you are still not happy with the price, you may just say so and stop the haggling.

FACE TO FACE

A أريد شراء ثوبا أزرق
u-rii-du shi-raa-a thaw-ban az-raq
I would like to buy that blue dress

B ما مقاسك؟
maa ma-qaa-su-ka
What is your size?

A المقاس
al-ma-qaas 40
Size 40

Shopping

Where are the shops?	أين المحلات؟ ay-nal ma-hal-laat?
I'm looking for...	أنا أبحث عن... anaa ab-ha-thu 'an...
Where is the nearest...?	أين أقرب...؟ ayna aq-rabu...?
Where is the nearest baker's?	أين أقرب خبّاز؟ ayna aq-ra-bu khab-baaz?

Where is the bazaar?	أين السّوق؟ aynas-suuq?
Is it open?	هل هو مفتوح؟ hal hu-wa maf-tuuh?
When does it close?	متى يغلق؟ ma-taa yaq-liq?
Can I take that one?	هل يمكن أن آخذ هذا؟! hal yum-ki-nu an aa-khu-tha haa-thaa?
How much is it?	بكّم هو؟ bi-kam hu-wa?
It's too expensive	إنّه غالي جدّاً in-na-hu qaa-lin jid-dan
I don't want it	لا أريده laa u-rii-duh

Shops

Where is the...? أين...؟ ayna...?

baker's	الخبّاز	al-khab-baaz
bookshop	المكتبة	al-mak-ta-ba
butcher's	الجزّار	al-Jaz-zaar
cake shop	محلّ الكعك	ma-hal-lul ka'k
clothes shop	محلّ الملابس	ma-hal-lul ma-laa-bis
gift/souvenir shop	هدايا/تذكارات	ha-daa-yaa/ ti-th-kaa-raat
greengrocer's	الخضريّ	al-khu-tha-ri
grocer's	البقّال	al-baq-qaal
hairdresser's	الحلاق	al-hal-laaq
jeweller's	الصّائغ	as-saa-iq
market	السّوق	as-suuq
newsagent's	بائع الصّحف	baa-i' as-su-huf
optician's	صانع النّظّارات	saa-ni' an-nath-thaa-raat
pharmacy	الصّيدليّة	as-say-da-li-yah
shoe shop	محلّ الحذاء	ma-hal-lul hi-thaa
shop	المحلّ	al-ma-hal
shopping centre	المركز التّجاريّ	al-mar-kaz at-ti-jaari

spice/herb shop	محلّ التوابل/ الأعشاب	ma-hal at-ta-waa-bil/al-a'-shaab
stationer's	المكتبة	al-mak-ta-ba
supermarket	سوبر ماركت	su-bar mar-kit
tobacconist's	بائع التّبغ	baa-I' at-tab-q
toy shop	محلّ اللّعب	ma-halul la'ib

Food (general)

You can buy most of these from a supermarket.

biscuits	البسكويتات	al-bas-ka-wii-taat
bread	الخبز	al-khubz
butter	الزّبدة	az-zub-da
cakes	الكعك	al-ka'k
cheese	الجبن	al-jub-n
chicken	الدّجاج	ad-da-jaa-j
chocolate	الشّوكولاتة	ash-shu-ku-laa-ta
coffee	القهوة	al-qah-wa
coffee (instant)	قهوة	qah-wa (Nescafé® nes-ka-fe)
crisps	شرائح البطاطس	sha-raa-ih al-ba-taa-tis
egg	بيضة	bay-da
fish	سمك	sa-mak

Food (general)

flour	دقيق	da-qii-q
honey	عسل	'a-sal
jam	مربى	mu-rab-baa
margarine	زبدة	zub-da
marmalade	مربى	mu-rab-baa
milk	لبن/حليب	la-ban/ha-liib
olive oil	زيت الزّيتون	zay-tuz-zay-tuun
orange juice	عصير البرتقال	'a-sii-rul bur-tu-qaal
pasta	المكرونة	al-ma-ka-roo-na
pepper (seasoning)	الفلفل (التّتبيل)	al-fil-fil (at-tat-biil)
rice	الأرز	al-aruz
salt	الملح	al-mal-h
stock cubes	المرق	al-ma-ra-q
sugar	السّكّر	as-suk-kar
tea	الشّاي	ash-shaa-y
vinegar	الخلّ	al-khal
yoghurt	الزّبادي	az-za-baa-dii

Shopping

Food (fruit and veg)

apples	التّفّاح	at-tuf-faah
apricots	المشمش	al-mish-mish

> **Measurements and quantities** (p 133)

aubergine	الباذنجان	al-baa-thin-jaan
bananas	الموز	al-mawz
cabbage	الكرنب	al-kar-nab
carrots	الجزر	al-ja-zar
cauliflower	القرنبيط	al-qar-na-biid
cherries	الكرز	al-ka-raz
courgettes	الكوسا	al-kuu-saa
cucumber	الخيار	al-kha-yaar
dates	التمر	at-tam-r
figs	التّين	at-tiin
garlic	الثّوم	ath-thawm
grapefruit	الجريبفروت	al-grape-fruut
grapes	العنب	al-'i-nab
green beans	الفاصولية الخضراء	al-faa-suu-liy-yah al-khad-raa
lemon	اللّيمون	al-lay-muun
lettuce	الخسّ	al-khas
melon	الشّمّام	ash-sham-maam
mushrooms	عيش الغراب	'esh al-quraab
nectarines	الخوخ	al-khuu-kh
onions	البصل	al-ba-sal
oranges	البرتقال	al-bur-tu-qaal
peaches	الخوخ	al-khuu-kh
pears	الكمّثرى	al-kum-mith-raa
peas	البسلّة	al-ba-sil-lah
peppers	الفلفل	al-fil-fil

pineapple	الأناناس	al-ana-naas
plums	البرقوق	al-bar-quuq
pomegranate	الرمّان	ar-rum-maan
potatoes	البطاطس	al-ba-taa-tis
sour-cherries	الكرز الحمضي	al-ka-raz al-him-thi
spinach	السّبانخ	as-sa-baa-nikh
strawberries	الفراولة	al-fa-raa-wila
tomatoes	الطّماطم	at-ta-maa-tim
watermelon	البطّيخ	al-bat-tiikh

Clothes

European sizes are the most commonly used, however, due to some products being imported from various parts of the world, other size guides may be found in some places.

women's sizes		men's suit sizes		shoe sizes			
UK	EU	UK	EU	UK	EU	UK	EU
10	40	36	46	2	35	7	41
12	42	38	48	3	36	8	42
14	44	40	50	4	37	9	43
16	46	42	52	5	38	10	44
18	48	44	54	6	39	11	45
20	50	46	56				

FACE TO FACE

A هل يمكن أن أقيس هذا؟

hal yum-kinu an a-qii-sa haa-thaa

Can I try this one on?

B نعم، بالطّبع، يمكن أن تقيسه هنا

na'am, bit-tab', yum-kinu an ta-qii-sa hu hu-naa

Yes, of course, you can try it on in here

A هل عندك هذا في الصغير

hal 'in-da-ka haa-thaa fis-sa-qiir

Do you have this one in a small size?

B نعم، موجود

na-'am, maw-juud

Yes, we do.

لا، غير موجود

laa, qayr maw-juud

No, we don't.

Clothes

Small صغير sa-qiir

Medium وسط wa-sat

Large كبير ka-biir

Is it real leather? هل هذا من جلد حقيقي؟
hal haa-thaa min jild ha-qii-qii?

Do you have this one in other colours? هل لديك هذا بلون آخر؟
hal la-day-ka haa-thaa bi-lawn aa-khar?

It's too expensive إنه غالي جدا
in-na-hu qaa-li jid-dan

It's too big إنه كبير جدا
in-na-hu ka-biir jid-dan

It's too small إنه صغير جدا
in-na-hu sa-qiir jid-dan

No thanks, I don't want it لا شكرا، لا أريده
laa shuk-ran, laa u-rii-duh

Clothes (articles)

cotton	القطن	al-qutn
leather	الجلد	al-jild

> **Paying** (p 108) > **Numbers** (p 134)

silk	الحرير	al-ha-riir
wool	الصوف	as-suuf
coat	المعطف	al-mi'-taf
dress	اللباس	al-li-baas
hat	القبعة	al-qub-ba-'a
jacket	السترة	as-sut-rah
knickers	الكلسون	al-kal-soon
sandals	الصنادل	as-sin-daal
shirt	القميص	al-qa-miis
shorts	سروال قصير	sir-waal qa-siir
skirt	التنورة	at-tan-nuu-ra
socks	الجوارب	al-ja-waa-rib
swimsuit	كسوة السباحة	kis-wat si-baa-ha
t-shirt	الفانيلة	al-faa-nil-la
trousers	البنطلون	al-ban-ta-loon
underpants	الملابس الداخلية	al-ma-laa-bis ad-daa-khi-liy-yah

Maps and guides

Unfortunately it is very difficult to find functional, well-designed maps in most Arab countries. The local tourist information office will usually be able to direct you. The word for map is kha-rii-ta.

Where can I buy a map?	أين يمكن لي أن أشتري خارطة؟ ay-na yum-kinu lii an ash-ta-ri-ya khaa-ri-ta?
Do you have a road map?	هل لديك خارطة طريق؟ hal la-day-ka khaa-ri-da-tu da-riiq?
Do you have a town plan?	هل لديك خارطة القرية؟ hal la-day-ka khaa-ri-da-tul-qar-yah?
Do you have a leaflet in English?	هل لديك منشورة hal la-day-ka man-shuu-rah bil in-gi-lii-ziy-yah
Do you have a guidebook in English?	دليل بالإنجليزية؟ hal la-day-ka da-liil bil in-gi-lii-ziy-yah?
Can you show me where ... is on the map?	تستطيع أن ترني مكان ... على الخارطة؟ tas-ta-dii' an tu-ri-nii ma-kaa-na ... 'a-laal-khaa-ri-da?

> **Asking the way** (p 30)

Where can I buy a newspaper? أين أستطيع شراء جريدة؟
ay-na as-ta-dii-'u shi-raa ja-rii-dah?

Have you any newspapers in English? هل لديك أي جرائد انجليزية؟
hal la-day-ka ay-yu ja-raa-id in-gil-lii-ziy-yah?

Post office

Post offices are usually open six days a week, being closed on Fridays.

البريد الجوي al-ba-riid al-jaw-wi	airmail
في الخارج fillkhaa-rij	overseas
داخل البلاد daa-khil al-bil-laad	inland
محلي ma-hal-lii	local
الرسالة ar-ra-saa-il	letter
البطاقة البريدية al-bi-taa-qa al-ba-rii-diy-yah	postcard
الطوابع at-ta-waa-bi'	stamps

Post office

Where is the post office?	أين مكتب البريد؟ ay-na mak-ta-bul-ba-riid?
Where can I buy stamps?	أين أشتري الطوابع؟ ay-na ash-ta-rii ad-da-waa-bi'?
five stamps	خمسة طوابع kham-su da-waa-bi'
10 stamps	عشرة طوابع 'ash-ra-tu da-waa-bi'
for postcards	للبطاقات البريدية lil-bi-taa-qaat al ba-rii-diy-yah
for letters	للرسائل lir-ra-saa-il
to Britain	إلى بريطانيا ilaa bri-taa-ni-yaa
to America	إلى أمريكا ilaa am-rii-kaa
to Australia	إلى أستراليا ilaa us-tu-raa-li-yaa

to Canada	الى كندا ilaa kanada

Photos

colour film	فلم ملون fi-lim mu-law-wan
Where is a photographic shop?	أين دكان التصوير؟ ay-na duk-kaa-nut-tas-wiir?
I need a film for this camera	أنا بحاجة إلى فلم لهذه الكاميرا ana bi-haa-ja ilaa fi-lim li haa-thi-hii al-kaa-mi-ra
I need a memory card for this camera	أنا بحاجة لبطاقة ذاكرة لهذه الكامرا ana bi-haa-ja ilaa bi-taa-qat thaa-ki-ra li haa-thi-hii al-kaa-mi-ra
I need batteries for this	أنا بحاجة إلى بطاريات لهذه ana bi-haa-ja ilaa bat-taa-riy-yaat li-haa-thi-hi

I'd like these films developed	أنا أودّ أن أحمض هذه الأفلام anaa a-wad-du an u-ham-mida haa-thi-hii al af-laam
How long will it take?	كم يأخذ هذا؟ kam ya-khu-thu haa-thaa?
How much will it cost?	كم ثمنها؟ kam tha-ma-nu-haa?

Leisure

Sightseeing and tourist office

Tourist offices provide lists of places to stay. In some countries like Egypt you will also find maps and leaflets describing local attractions.

استعلامات is-ti'-laa-maat	information
المكتب السياحي a-mak-tab as-si-yaa-hii	tourist office
المتحف al-mit-haf	museum
المعرض الفني al-ma'-rad al-fan-nii	art gallery
مسجد mas-jid	mosque
الجولة المنظمة al-jaw-la al-mu-na-tha-ma	guided tour
التذاكر at-ta-thaa-kir	tickets
الحمام/مرحاض al-ham-maam/mir-haa-th	toilet

Where is the tourist office?	اين المكتب السياحي؟ ay-nal mak-tab as-si-yaa-hi?
What can we visit in the area?	ما الذي يمكننا زيارته في المنطقة؟ mal-la-thii yum-ki-nu-naa zi-yaa-ra-tu-hu fil-man-ti-qa?
Have you got details in English?	هل لديك التفاصيل باللغة الإنجليزية؟ hal la-day-ka at-ta-faa-siil bil-lu-qal-in-gi-lii-ziy-yah?
Are there any excursions?	هل هناك أيّ نزهات؟ hal hu-naa-ka ay-yu nu-zu-haat?
When does it leave?	متى ستقلع؟ ma-taa sa-tuq-li'?
When does it get back?	متى ستعود؟ ma-taa sa-ta-'uud?

> **Maps and guides** (p 75)

Entertainment

What is there to do in the evenings? ماذا هناك للقيام به في أمسيات ؟
ma-thaa hu-naa-ka lil-qi-yaam bi-hi fil-um-siy-yaat?

We would like to go to a disco نحن نودّ أن نذهب إلى دسكو
nah-nu na-wad-du an nath-ha-ba ilad-disko

Is there anywhere we can go to hear live music? هل هناك أي مكان يمكن أن نذهبه لنسمع موسيقى حيّة؟
hal hu-naaka ay-yu ma-kaan yum-ki-nu an nath-ha-ba-hu li-sa-maa-l mu-sii-qaa hay-ya?

Is there anywhere we can go to see belly-dancing? هل هناك أيّ مكان يمكن أن نذهب لرؤية الرقص الشرقي؟
hal hu-naa-ka ay-yu ma-kaan yum-ki-nu an nath-ha-ba li-ru-yat ar-raq-sa ash-sharqii?

Is there any entertainment for children? هل هناك أيّ ترفيه للأطفال؟
hal-hu-naa-ka ay-yu tar-fiih lil-at-faal?

Entertainment

Leisure/beach

شاطئ shaa-ti	beach
خطر kha-tar	danger
أدشاش ad-shaa-sh	showers

Are there any good beaches around here?

هل هناك أيّ شواطئ جيدة في هذه النواحي؟
hal hu-naa-ka ay-yu sha-waa-ti jay-yi-da fil haa-thi-hin-na-waa-hii?

Is there a bus to the beach?

هل هناك حافلة الى الشاطئ؟
hal hu-naa-ka haa-fila ilash-shaa-ti?

Is there a shared taxi to the beach?

هل هناك سيارة أجرة جماعية للشاطئ؟
hal hu-naa-ka say-yaa-rat uj-rah ja-maa-'iy-yah ilash-shaa-ti?

Can we go windsurfing?

هلّ بالإمكان أن نذهب لركوب الأمواج ؟
hal bil-im-kaa-ni an nath-ha-ba li-ru-kuu-bil am-waaj?

Please go away!	من فضلك اتركني! min fad-lak ut-ruk-nii!

Music

Is there anywhere we can go to hear Arabic music?	هل هناك أي مكان يمكن أن نذهب لسماع موسيقى عربية؟ hal hu-naa-ka ay-yu ma-kaan yum-ki-nu an nath-ha-ba li-sa-maa-'i mu-sii-qaa 'a-ra-biy-ya?
Are there any concerts?	هل هناك أيّ حفلات موسيقية؟ hal hu-naa-ka ay-yu ha-fa-laat muu-sii-qiy-yah?
Where can I get tickets?	أين أحصل على التذاكر؟ ay-na ah-su-lu alat-ta-thaa-kir?
Where can I hear some classical music?	أين يمكن أن أسمع بعض الموسيقى الكلاسيكية ay-na yum-ki-nu an as-ma-'a ba'-thal-muu-sii-qaa al-ka-laa-sii-kiy-yah

> **Making friends** (p 24)

Where can I hear some jazz?

أين يمكن أن أسمع بعض موسيقى الجاز؟
ay-na yum-ki-nu an as-ma-'a ba'-thal-muu-sii-qaa al-jaaz?

Cinema

سنما si-ni-ma	cinema
عرض 'ar-th	screening

What's on at the cinema?

ماذا في السينما؟
maa-thaa fis-si-ni-maa?

What time does the film start?

أيّ وقت يبدأ الفلم؟
fii ay-yi waq-tin yab-da-ul filim?

How much are the tickets?

ما قيمة التذاكر؟
maa qii-ma-tut-ta-thaa-kir?

Two for the (give name and time of performance) showing

إثنان لعرض...
ith-naan li-'ar-dth (...)

YOU MAY HEAR...	
لعرض ... ليس لدينا تذاكر متبقية li-'ard ... lay-sa la-day-naa ta-thaa-kir mu-ta-baq-qi-yah	We have no tickets for the ... screening

Mosque

Women should have their head covered and both men and women should avoid wearing shorts. You will have to leave your shoes at the entrance. Prayers take place five times a day and it is best to wait until these have finished before entering.

مسجد mas-jid	mosque
مسلم mus-lim	Muslim
مسيحي ma-sii-hi	Christian
حذاء hi-thaa	shoes
ممنوع التصوير mam-nuu' at-tas-wiir	no photos
ممنوع التصوير mam-nuu' at-tas-wiir	no videos

I'd like to see the mosque
أنا أودّ أن أرى المسجد
anaa a-wad-du an a-raal mas-jid

When can we see the mosque?
متى بالإمكان أن نرى المسجد؟
ma-taa bil-im-kaa-ni an na-raa al mas-jid?

Where is the mosque?
أين المسجد؟
ay-nal mas-jid?

Television

Most Arab countries have state channels which broadcast in Arabic, with films shown in the original language and subtitled. Besides that, other channels broadcast in English for the English speaking viewers and you will find news in English, and Western films. Most hotels and bars have satellite TV.

جهاز التحكّم عن بعد ji-haaz at-ta-hak-kum min bu'-d	remote control
الأخبار al-akh-baar	news
للتشغيل lit-tash-qiil	to switch on
للإطفاء lil-it-faa	to switch off
رسوم متحركة ru-suum mu-ta-har-rika	cartoons

Where is the television? أين التلفزيون؟
ay-nal ti-li-fiz-yoon?

How do I switch on the television? كيف أشغّل التلفزيون؟
kay-fa u-sh-'ilu at-ti-li-fiz-yoon?

What's on television? ماذا يعرض على التلفزيون؟
maa-thaa yu'-radu 'a-lat-tilifiz-yoon?

Are there any channels in English? هل هناك أيّ قنوات باللغة الإنجليزية؟
hal hu-naa-ka ay-yu qa-na-waat bil-luqal in-gi-lii-ziy-yah?

Are there any children's programmes?	هل هناك أيّ برامج للأطفال؟ hal hu-naa-ka ay-yu ba-raa-mij lil-at-faal?
When is the football on?	متى تكون كرة القدم الأخبارعلى الشاشة؟ ma-taa ta-kuu-nu ku-rat al-qa-dam 'a-lash-shaa-shah?
When is the news on?	متى تكون الأخبارعلى الشاشة؟ ma-taa ta-kuu-nu al-akh-baar 'a-lash-shaa-shah?

Sport

Where can we play tennis?	أين يمكننا أن نلعب التنس؟ ay-na yum-ki-nu-naa an nal-'a-ba at-ta-nis?
Where can we play golf?	أين يمكننا أن نلعب جولف؟ ay-na yum-ki-nu-naa an nal-'a-ba golf?
Where can we play football?	أين يمكننا أن نلعب كرة القدم؟ ay-na yum-ki-nu-naa an nal-'a-ba ku-rat al qa-dam?

Can we play tennis?	هلّ بالإمكان أن نلعب التنس؟ hal bi-im-kaa-ni-naa an nal-'a-ba at-ta-nis?
Can we play golf?	هلّ بالإمكان أن نلعب جولف؟ hal bi-im-kaa-ni-naa an nal-'a-ba golf?
Can we hire rackets?	هلّ بالإمكان أن نستأجر المضارب؟ hal bil-im-kaani an nas-ta-ji-ra al-ma-thaa-rib?
Can we hire golf clubs?	هلّ بالإمكان أن نستأجر عصى الجولف؟ hal bil-im-kaani an nas-ta-ji-ra a-saal-golf?
How much is it per hour?	كم سعره بالسّاعة؟ kam si'-ru-hu bis-saa'ah?
Can we watch a football match?	هلّ بالإمكان أن نشاهد مباراة كرة القدم؟ hal bil-im-kaa-ni an nu-shaa-hida mu-baa-raat ku-rat al-qa-dam?

Where can we get tickets? أين نحصل على التذاكر؟
ay-na nah-si-lu 'a-laat-ta-thaa-kir?

How do we get to the stadium? كيف نصل إلى الملعب؟
kay-fa na-si-lu ilal-mal-'ab?

Turkish baths

Turkish baths are commonly known and available in all Arab countries. A wide variety of treatments and facilities such as saunas and Turkish baths are on offer, and they are easy to find in most hotels in big cities. There are separate times or days for men and women. You are given a couple of towels and wooden bath clogs, and shown to the changing room to undress. Wearing a towel (or swimming costume if the bath-house is mixed) you are shown to a cubicle in the steamy marble washroom. Here, buckets of hot water are poured over you, before you lie on a circular hot marble slab and an attendant rubs your skin with a coarse cloth until your skin glows. You will be finished off with a rinse and a massage.

الحمّامات التركية al-ham-maa-maat at-tur-kiy-yah	Turkish baths
الرجال ar-ri-jaal	men
النساء an-ni-saa	women
حار haar	hot
بارد baa-rid	cold
الصابون as-saa-buun	soap
المنشفة al-min-sha-fa	towel
الليفة al-lii-fa	loofah
نعال الحمّام ni-'aal-ul-ham-maam	bath clogs
قفاز الفرك الخشن quf-faaz al-fark al-kha-shin	coarse rubbing-glove

Where are the baths? — أين الحمّامات؟
ay-nal ham-maa-maat?

Where do I undress? — أين أنزع الملابس؟
ay-na an-zi-'ul ma-laa-bis?

Is the hamam only for women or is it mixed?	هل الحمام للنساء فقط أم مختلط؟ hal al-ham-maa-mu lin-ni-saa fa-qat am mukh-ta-lad?
I would like a massage	أريد تدليك u-rii-du tad-liik
Where is the steam room?	أين غرفة البخار؟ ay-na qur-fa-tul bu-khaar?

Walking

Are there any guided walks?	هل هناك جولات مع دليل؟ hal hu-naa-ka jaw lat ma da lil?
Do you have a guide to local walks?	هل لديك دليل إلى أماكن التجول المحليّ؟ hal la-day-ka da-liil ilaa amaa-kin at-ta-jaw-wul al ma-hal-li?

How many kilometres is the walk?	كم عدد كيلومترات الجولة؟ kam 'a-dad kilo-mit-raat al-jaw-lah?
How long will it take?	كم من الوقت يأخذ؟ kam min al-waq-ti ya-khuth?
Is it very steep?	هل هو منحدر جدا؟ hal hu-wa mun-ha-dir jid-dan?
I'd like to go climbing	أودّ أن أذهب للتسلّق awad-du an ath-ha-ba lit-ta-sal-luq

> **Maps and guides** (p 75)

Communications

Telephone and mobile

If you plan to make international calls, a phonecard is the most convenient way of paying for them. To phone Egypt, the international code is 00 20 plus the Egyptian area code followed by the number. Please check the international access code for your destination.

عملة الهاتف 'um-lat al-haa-tif	phone token
بطاقة الهاتف bi-taa-qat al-haa-tif	phonecard
دليل الهاتف da-liil al-haa-tif	telephone directory
(الدفع العكسي) كلكت ad-daf' al-'ak-si	reverse charges (collect)
رمز الإتصال الهاتفي ramz al-it-ti-saal al-haa-ti-fi	dialling code

FACE TO FACE

A مرحبا...
marhaba...
Hello

B مرحبا، هذا... أودّ أن أتكلّم مع...
mar-haba, haa-thaa... awad-du an ata-kal-lama ma'a...
Hello, this is... I would like to speak to...

A ثانية واحدة
thaa-ni-yah waa-hi-da
Just a second

I want to make a phone call
أريد إجراء مكالمة هاتفية
urii-du ij ra'a mu-kaa-la-mah haa-ti-fiy-yah

I want to phone the UK
أريد أن أتصل بالمملكة المتحدة
urii-du an at-tasila bil-mam-laka al-mut-ta-hi-da

I want to phone Canada
أريد أن أتصل بكندا
urii-du an at-tasila bikanada

I want to phone Australia
أريد أن اتصل بأستراليا
urii-du an at-tasila biustralia

I want to phone the USA	أريد أن أتصل بأمريكا urii-du an at-tasila biamerica
An outside line, please	خط خارجي، رجاء khat khaa-ri-ji, ra-jaa-an
Where can I buy a phonecard?	أين أشتري بطاقة الهاتف؟ ay-na ash-ta-rii bi-taa-qat-tul-haa-tif?
Please write the phone number down	رجاء إكتب رقم الهاتف ra-jaa-an uk-tub ra-qam al-haa-tif
Do you have a mobile phone?	هل لديك هاتف جوّال؟ hal la-day-ka haa-tif jaw-waal?
Can I speak to...	هل من الممكن أن أتكلم مع... hal minal-mum-kin an ata-kal-lama ma-'a...
This is...	هذا... haa-thaa...
I'll call back later	سأعيد الإتصال لاحقا sa-u-'ii-du al-it-ti-saa-la laa-hi-qan

I'll call again tomorrow	سأتّصل ثانية غدا sa-at-ta-silu thaa-ni-ya-tan qa-dan	

YOU MAY HEAR...	
مرحبا mar-haba	Hello
لحظة لو سمحت lah-tha law sa-maht	Please hold on
من المتصل؟ man-nil mut-ta-sil?	Who is calling?
هلّ بالإمكان أن تتصل لاحقا؟ hal bil-im-kaan an tat-ta-sila laa-hi-qan?	Can you call back later?
هل تريد ترك رسالة؟ hal tu-rii-du tar-ka ri-saa-lah?	Do you want to leave a message?
الرقم غلط ar-ra-qam qa-lad	Wrong number
جهاز الإجابة الآلي ji-haaz al ija ba al ali	Answering machine

Text messaging

SMS is a very popular communication tool.

I will text you	سأبعث إليك رسالة sa-ab-'a-thu ilay-ka ri-saa-lah
Can you text me?	هلّ بالإمكان أن ترسل إلي رسالة؟ hal bil-im-kaa-ni an tur-sila ilay-ya ri-saa-la?
Did you get my text message?	هل وجدت رسالتي؟ hal wa-jat-ta ri-saa-la-tii?
Can you send me a picture with your mobile?	هل تستطيع أن ترسل إلي صورة بجوالك ؟ hal tas-ta-dii-'u an tur-sila ilay-ya suu-ra-tan bi-jaw-waa-lak?
Hello	مرحبا mar-haba
Hello (to answer the phone)	مرحبا/ألو mar-haba/alo

See you	أراك لاحقا araa-ka laa-hi-qan
Tomorrow	غدا qa-dan
Please call me	رجاء إتّصل بي ra-jaa-an it-tasil bii
Today	اليوم al-yawm
Too late	متأخر جدا mu-ta-akhir jid-dan
Tonight	الليلة al-lay-la
Text me	راسلني raa-sil-nii
Free to talk?	هل تستطيع الكلام؟ hal tas-ta-dii-'ul ka-laam?
I will call you back later	سأتّصل بك لاحقا sa-at-ta-si-lu bi-ka laa-hi-qan

Thanks	شكرا shuk-ran
Are you ok?	هل أنت بخير؟ hal anta bi-khayr?

E-mail

Almost every country has its own top-level domain (TLD) which is the last part of an Internet domain name. For example, Egypt's is '**.eg**'; Morocco's is '**.mc**'; and Tunisia's is '**.tn**'). The '**.com**' domain is used in all the Arab countries.

Do you have e-mail?	هل لك بريد إلكتروني؟ hal la-ka ba-riid ilik-troo-ni?
My e-mail address is...	عنوان بريدي الإلكتروني... 'un-waa-nu ba-rii-dii al-ilik-trooni...
What is your e-mail address?	ما هو عنوان بريدك الإلكتروني؟ ma hu-wa 'un-waa-nu ba-rii-da-kal ilik-trooni?

Communications

How do you spell it?	كيف تهجيه؟ kay-fa tu-haj-jiih?
All one word	كلها كلمة واحدة kul-lu-haa ka-li-mah waa-hi-da
All lower case	جميعها حروف صغيرة ja-mii-'u-haa hu-ruuf-sa-qii-ra
Can I send an e-mail?	هل وصلك بريدي الإلكتروني؟ hal wa-sa-la-ka ba-rii-dii al ilik-troo-ni?
Did you get my e-mail?	هل وصلك البريد الإلكتروني مني؟ hal wa-sa-la-ka ba-rii-dii al ilik-troo-ni?

Internet

Most computer terminology tends to be in English. Internet cafés are widespread and very popular.

home	الصفحة الرئيسية	as-saf-ha ar-ra-ii-siy-yah
username	اسم المستعمل	ismul-mus-takh-dim
to browse	يتصفح	ya ta sa fah
search engine	وسيلة البحث	was ilat el ba hath
password	كلمة السر	ka-li-mat as-sir
contact us	اتّصل بنا	it-tasil bi-naa
back to menu	عد إلى القائمة	'ud ilal-qaa-i-mah
sitemap	خريطة الموقع	kha ritat el maw qi

Are there any Internet cafés here?
هل هناك أيّ مقاهي الإنترنت هنا؟
hal hu-naa-ka ay-yu ma-qaa-hii inter-net hu-naa?

How much is it to log on for an hour?
كم سعر الإتّصال بشبكت الانترنت لساعة؟
kam si'-rul it-ti-saal bi sha-ba-kat al-inter-net li-saa-'ah?

I would like to print some pages	أودّ أن أطبع بعض الصفحات awad-du an ad-ba-'a ba'-thas-sa-fa-haat

Fax

To send a fax to Egypt, the international code is 00 20 plus the Egyptian area code (e.g. 2) followed by the number.

من min	from
إلى ilaa	to
التأريخ at-taa-riikh	date
صفحات بتضمين هذه... ...sa-fa-haat bi-that-miin haa-thih	...pages including this

I want to send a fax	أريد إرسال فاكس u-rii-du ir-saa-la fax
Do you have a fax?	هل لديك فاكس؟ hal la-day-ka faa-ks?

Where can I send a fax? | أين أستطيع أن أرسل فاكس؟
ay-na as-ta-dii-'u an ur-si-la fak-san?

How much is it to send a fax? | كم سعر إرسال الفاكس؟
kam si'-ru ir-saa-lil-faa-ks?

What is your fax number? | ما رقم فاكسك؟
maa ra-qa-mu faak-si-ka?

The fax number is... | رقم الفاكس هو...
ra-qa-mul-faa-ks hu-wa...

Practicalities

Money

Banks are closed on Fridays. The best place to change money is at a المصرف **Al Masraf** or bureau de change. If there is no bureau de change around, jewellery shops can also change money. It is easier to change cash than traveller's cheques in some countries, but in more tourist orientated countries traveller's cheques are not a problem at all. The Egyptian currency is the Egyptian pound, the Moroccan currency is the dirham and the Tunisian currency is the Tunisian dinar.

Where is the nearest bank? — أين أقرب بنك؟ ay-na aq-ra-bu bank?

Where is the nearest bureau de change? — أين أقرب مكتب صرافة؟ ay-na aq-ra-bu mak-tab sar-raa-fah?

Can I change money here?	هل بالإمكان أن أصرف نقودا هنا؟ hal bil-im-kaan an as-ri-fa nu-quu-dan hu-naa?
What is the exchange rate?	ما سعر الصرف؟ maa si'-rus-sar-raa-fah?
I want to change £50	أريد صرف ٥٠£ u-rii-du sar-fa ٥٠£
I want to change traveller's cheques	أريد صرف صكوك المسافرين (فقط في البنوك) u-rii-du sar-fa su-kuuk al-mu-saa-fi-riin

Paying

Credit cards are becoming more widely accepted. Service charges are included in restaurants, bars and cafés, but a tip is still customary. It is, however, a good idea to have cash on you when buying things.

الفاتورة al-faa-tuu-ra	bill
الإيصال al-ii-saal	receipt
الفاتورة al-faa-tuu-ra	invoice
نقطة الدفع nuq-dat ad-daf'	cash desk
بطاقة الإئتمان bi-taa-qat al-i-ti-maan	credit card

I'd like to pay now
أودّ أن أدفع الآن
a-wad-du an ad-fa-'a al-aan

How much is it?
كم المبلغ؟
kam al-mab-laq?

Can I pay... ?
هلّ بالإمكان أن أدفع...
hal bil-im-kaa-ni an ad-fa-'a...

by credit card
بالبطاقة الائتمانية
bil-bitaa-qa al-i-ti-maa-niy-ya

with traveller's cheques
بصكوك المسافرين
bi-su-kuuk al-mu-saa-fi-riin

Can I pay by cheque?
هلّ بالإمكان أن أدفع بشيك (صك)؟
hal bil-im-kaa-ni an ad-fa-'a shiik (sak)?

Paying

Where do I pay?	أين أدفع؟ ay-na ad-fa'?
Please write down the price	رجاء إكتب السعر ra-jaa-an uk-tub as-si'r
Put it on my bill (in hotel)	ضعه على فاتورتي في (الفندق) da'-hu 'a-laa faa-tuu-ra-tii (fil-fun-duq)
I'd like a receipt, please	أودّ إيصالا، رجاء a-wad-du ii-saa-lan, ra-jaa-an
I think there is a mistake	أعتقد أن هناك خطأ a'-ta-qi-du an-na hu-naa-ka kha-ta
Keep the change	إحتفظ بالباقي ih-ta-fid bil-baa-qii

Luggage

الحقيبة al-ha-qii-ba	suitcase
حقيبة يدوية ha-qii-ba ya-da-qiy-yah	handbag
الحقيبة al-ha-qii-ba	briefcase
الأمتعة اليدوية al-am-ti-‘a al-ya-da-wy-yah	hand luggage
مكتب إيداع الحقائب mak-tab ii-daa’ al-ha-qaa-ib	left luggage office
الخزانة al-khaz-nah	locker
العربة al-‘a-ra-bah	trolley

My suitcase hasn't arrived
حقيبتي ما وصلت
ha-qii-ba-tii maa wa-sa-lat

My suitcase is missing
حقيبتي مفقودة
ha-qii-ba-tii maf-quu-dah

My suitcase is damaged
حقيبتي متضرّرة
ha-qii-ba-tii mu-ta-dar-ri-rah

> **Train** (p 37) > **Air travel** (p 45)

Can I leave my suitcase here? | هلّ بالإمكان أن أترك حقيبتي هنا؟
hal bil-im-kaa-ni an at-ru-ka ha-qii-ba-tii hu-naa?

Is there a left luggage office? | هل هناك مكتب إيداع الحقائب؟
hal hu-naa-ka mak-tab ii-daa' al-ha-qaa-ib?

When does it open? | متى يفتح؟
ma-taa yaf-tah?

When does it close? | متى يغلق؟
ma-taa yuq-liq?

Repairs

دكان تصليح الحذاء duk-kaan tas-liih al-hi-thaa	shoe repair shop
التصليحات بينما تنتظر at-tas-lii-haat bay-na-maa tan-ta-thir	repairs while you wait

Where can I get this repaired?	أين أستطيع أن أصلح هذا؟ ay-na as-ta-dii-'u an u-sal-li-ha haa-thaa?
This is broken	هذا مكسور haa-thaa mak-suur
Can you repair...?	هلْ تستطيع تصليح...؟ hal tas-ta-dii-'u tas-lii-ha...?
my glasses?	نظاراتي؟ nath-thaa-raa-tii?
my camera?	آلة تصويري (كامرتي)؟ aa-lat tas-wii-rii (kee-ma-ra-tii)?
How much will it cost?	كم ستكلّف؟ kam sa-tu-kal-lif?
How long will it take?	كم من الوقت يأخذ؟ kam min al-waq-ti ya-khu-th?

Repairs

> **Breakdown** (p 52)

Laundry

مسحوق الغسيل mas-huuq al-qa-siil	washing powder
مغسلة maq-sa-lah	launderette
المنظف الجاف al-mu-na-thif al-jaaf	dry-cleaner's

Where can I wash some clothes?
أين أغسل بعض الملابس؟
ay-na aq-si-lu ba'-thal-ma-laa-nis?

Do you have a laundry service?
هل لديك خدمة تغسيل الملابس؟
hal la-day-ka khid-mat taq-siil al-ma-laa-bis?

Where is the launderette?
أين محل غسل الملابس؟
ay-na ma-hal qa-siil al-ma-laa-bis?

Where is the dry-cleaner's?
أين المنظف الجاف؟
ay-na al-mu-na-thiful-jaaf?

Can I borrow an iron?	هلّ بإمكاني أن أستعير مكواتك؟ hal bi-im-kaa-nii an as-ta-'ii-ra mik-waa-tak?

YOU MAY HEAR...	
لكلٌ واحده li-kul-li waa-hi-da	per item

Complaints

This doesn't work	هذا لا يعمل haa-thaa laa ya'-mal
The room is dirty	إنّ الغرفة قذرة in-nal-qur-fah qa-thi-ra
The room is too hot	إنّ الغرفة حارة جدا in-nal-qur-fah haar-rah jid-dan
The room is too cold	إنّ الغرفة بارده جدا in-nal-qur-fah baa-ri-dah jid-dan
I didn't order this	أنا لم أطلب هذا anaa lam at-lub haa-thaa

I want to complain	أريد الشكوى u-rii-dush-shak-waa
Please call the manager	رجاء إتّصل بالمدير ra-jaa-an it-ta-sil bil-mu-diir
...out of order	عاطل... ... 'aa-til
toilet	المرحاض al-mir-haad
shower	الدش ad-dush
television	التلفزيون at-ti-li-fiz-yoon

Practicalities

Problems

Can you help me?	هلّ بإمكانك أن تساعدني؟ hal bil-im-kaa-ni-ka an tu-saa-'i-da-nii?

> **Hotel desk** (p 60)

I don't speak Arabic	أنا لا أتكلّم اللغة العربية anaa laa at-ta-kal-la-mu al-lu-qa al-'a-ra-biy-ya
Do you speak English?	هل تتكلّم الانجليزية؟ hal ta-ta-kal-la-mu al-in-gi-lii-ziy-yah?
Is there someone who speaks English?	هل هناك من يتكلّم الانجليزية؟ hal hu-naa-ka man ya-ta-kal-la-mul-in-gi-lii-ziy-ya?
I'm lost	أنا تائه anaa taa-ih
I need to go to...	أريد الذهاب إلى... u-rii-du ath-tha-haa-ba ilaa...
the station	المحطة al-ma-**ħat-ta**
my hotel	فندقي **fun-du-qii**
this address	هذا العنوان **haa-th**aa al-'un-waan

Problems

I've missed my train	فوّت قطاري faw-wat-tu qi-taa-rii
I've missed my bus	فوّت حافلتي faw-wat-tu haa-fi-la-tii
I've missed my plane	فوّت طائرتي faw-wat-tu taa-i-ra-tii
I've missed the connection	فوّت الوصلة faw-wat-tu al-was-la
The coach has left without me	رحلت الحافلة بدونني ra-ha-lat haa-fi-la-tii bi-duu-nii
How does this work?	كيف يعمل هذا؟ kay-fa ya'-ma-lu haa-thaa?
That man is following me	ذلك الرجل يتبعني thaa-li-kar-ra-ju-lu yat-ba-'u-nii
I have lost my money	فقدت مالي fa-qat-tu maa-lii

Practicalities

Emergencies

الشرطة ash-shur-ta	police
اطفائية it-faa-iy-ya	fire brigade
سيارة الإسعاف say-yaa-rat is-‘aaf	ambulance
المستشفى al-mus-tash-faa	hospital
الحوادث و الطوارئ al-ha-waa-dith wat-ta-waa-ri	A&E

Help! — النجده!
an-naj-da!

Fire! — حريق!
ha-riiq!

There's been an accident — هناك حادث
hu-naa-ka haa-dith

Please help me — رجاء ساعدني
ra-jaa-an saa-‘id-nii

Please call the police	رجاء إتّصل بالشرطة ra-jaa-an it-ta-sil bish-shur-ta
Please call the fire brigade	رجاء إتّصل بالاطفائية ra-jaa-an it-ta-sil bi it-faa-iy-yah
Someone has been injured	شخص ما أصيب shakh-sun ma u-siib
Where is the police station?	أين مركز الشرطة؟ ay-na mar-kaz ash-shur-ta?
I've been robbed	لقد سرقت la-qad su-riqt
I've been raped	لقد إغتصبت la-qad iq-tu-sibt
I want to speak to a policewoman	أريد الكلام مع شرطية u-rii-dul-ka-laa-ma ma-'a shur-tiy-ya
Someone has stolen...	شخص سرق... shakh-sun sa-ra-qa...

I've lost...	فقدت... fa-qat-tu...
my money	مالي maa-lii
my passport	جواز سفري ja-waa-za sa-fa-rii
my air ticket	تذاكري ta-thaa-ki-rii
My son is missing	إبني مفقود ib-nii maf-quud
My daughter is missing	بنتي مفقودة bin-tii maf-quu-da
His/Her name is...	اسمه/اسمها... is-mu-hu/is-mu-haa...
I need a report for my insurance	أحتاج تقريرا لشركة التأمين ah-taa-ju taq-rii-ran li-sha-ri-kat at-ta-miin

Please call the British Embassy	رجاء إتّصل بالسفارة البريطانية ra-jaa-an it-ta-sil bis-sa-faa-rah al-bri-taa-niy-yah
Please call the Canadian Embassy	رجاء إتّصل بالسفارةالكندية ra-jaa-an it-ta-sil bis-sa-faa-rah al kanadiyah
Please call the American Embassy	رجاء إتّصل بالسفارة الأمريكية ra-jaa-an it-ta-sil bis-sa-faa-rah al-am-rii-kiy-yah
Please call the Australian Embassy	رجاء إتّصل بالسفارة الأسترالية ra-jaa-an it-ta-sil bis-sa-faa-rah alustraliah

Health

Pharmacy

Pharmacies صيدلية (say-da-liy-ya) keep the same hours as other shops. Pharmacists often speak some English.

أين أقرب صيدلية؟ ay-na aq-ra-bu say-da-liy-yah?	Where is the nearest pharmacy?

I need something...	أحتاج شيء... ah-taa-ju shay-an...
for diarrhoea	للإسهال lil is-haal
for constipation	للإمساك lil im-saak
for food poisoning	للتسمّم الغذائي lit-ta-sam-mum al-qi-thaa-ii

Is it safe for...? — هل هو آمن لـ ...؟
hal hu-wa aa-min li...?

children — الأطفال
al-at-faal

I am pregnant — أنا حامل
anaa haa-mil

What is the dose? — ما الجرعة؟
mal jur-'ah?

YOU MAY HEAR...	
3 مرات في اليوم 3 mar-raat fil yawm	three times a day
قبل/بعد الغذاء qab-la/ba'-da al-qa-daa	before/after food
مع الغذاء ma-'al qa-daa	with food

Health

Body

I have broken... إنكسرت...
in-ka-sa-rat...

my foot قدمي
qa-da-mii

my ankle كاحلي
kaa-hi-lii

my hand يدي
ya-dii

my arm ذراعي
thi-raa-'ii

It hurts تألمني
tu-li-mu-nii

Doctor

المستشفى al-mus-tash-faa	hospital
قسم الضحايا qis-muth-tha-haa-yaa	casualty department
الوصفة al-was-fa	prescription
سيارة الإسعاف say-yaa-tu is-'aaf	ambulance

FACE TO FACE

A أشعر بالتوعك
as'ur bi-ta wa' uk
I don't feel right

B هل عندك سخونة؟
hal 'in-da-ka su-khuu-na?
Do you have a temperature?

A لا. عندي ألم هنا
laa. 'in-dii alam hu-naa
No. I have a pain here

Health

I need to see a doctor — أحتاج لرؤية طبيب
ah-taa-ju il-ru-ya-ti ta-biib

My son/daughter is ill	إبني مريض/بنتي مريضة ib-nii/bin-tii ma-rii-tha
Will he have to go to hospital?	هل عليه أن يذهب إلى المستشفى؟ hal 'a-lay-hi an yath-ha-ba ilal-mus-tash-faa?
Will she have to go to hospital?	هل يجب عليها أن تذهب إلى المستشفى؟ hal ya-jibu 'a-lay-ha an tath-ha-ba ilal-mus-tash-faa?
I'm on the Pill	أنا أتناول حبوب منع الحمل anaa atanaa-wa-lu hu-buuba man'il-haml
I'm diabetic	أنا مريض بالسكر anaa ma-rii-th bis-suk-kar
I need insulin	أحتاج أنسيولين ah-taaj in-su-liin
I'm allergic to penicillin	عندي حسّاسية من البنسلين 'in-dii ha-saa-si-ya min al-bin-si-liin

Doctor

> **Emergencies** (p 119)

Will I have to pay? — هل يجب عليّ أن أدفع؟
hal ya-ji-bu 'a-lay-ya an ad-fa-'a?

Can you give me a receipt for the insurance? — هلّ بالإمكان أن تعطيني وصل إستلام للتأمين؟
hal bil-im-kaan an tu'-dii-nii wasl is-ti-laam lit-ta-miin?

Dentist

You will have to pay for dental work at the time of treatment, so be sure to ask for a receipt so that you can claim a refund from your holiday insurance. Make sure you choose a clean and well presented dentist.

الحشوة al-ha-sh-wa	filling
التاج at-taaj	crown
أطقم الأسنان at-qumul-as-naan	dentures
الحقن al-hu-qan	injection

Health

I need to go to a dentist	أحتاج للذهاب إلى طبيب أسنان ah-taaj lith-tha-haabi ilaa ta-bii-bi as-naan
He has toothache	هوعنده وجع أسنان hu-wa 'in-da-hu wa-ja' as-naan
She has toothache	هي عندها وجع أسنان hi-ya 'in-da-haa wa-ja' as-naan
This hurts	هذا يؤلم haa-thaa yu-li-mu
My filling has come out	حشوة سني خرج hash-wii kha-raj
My crown has come out	تاجي خرج taaj-jii kha-raj
Can you do emergency treatment?	هلّ بالإمكان أن تعمل معالجة مستعجلة؟ hal bil-im-kaa-ni an ta'-ma-la mu-'aa-la-ja mus-ta'-ji-la?

Different types of travellers

Disabled travellers

Is there a toilet for the disabled?	هل هناك مرحاض للمعوّقين؟ hal hu-naa-ka mir-haad lil-mu-'aw-wa-qiin?
I want a room on the ground floor	أريد غرفة على الطابق الأرضي u-rii-du qur-fa 'a-lat-taabiq al-ar-dii
Can I enter in a wheelchair?	هلّ بالإمكان أن أدخل في كرسي المعوقين؟ hal bil-im-kaan an ad-khu-la fii kur-siy-yil mu-'aw-wa-qiin?
Is there a lift?	هل هناك مصعد؟ hal hu-naa-ka mis-'ad?

> **Hotel (booking)** (p 56)

Where is the lift?	أين المصعد؟ ay-nal mis-'ad?
Is there a reduction for the disabled?	هل هناك تخفيض للمعوّقين؟ hal hu-naa-ka takh-fiid lil mu-'aw-wa-qiin?
I am deaf	أنا أصمّ anaa a-sam

With kids

A child's ticket	تذكرة لطفل that-ka-ra li-tifl
He is ... years old	هي عمرها... سنوات hi-ya 'um-ru-haa ... sa-na-waat
She is ... years old	هو عمره ... سنوات hu-wa 'um-ruhu ... sa-na-waat
Is there a reduction for children?	هل هناك تخفيض للأطفال؟ hal hu-naa-ka takh-fiid lil at-faal?

Do you have a children's menu? | هل لديكم قائمة أطفال؟
hal la-day-kum qaa-i-ma-tu at-faal?

Is it OK to take children? | هل من الممكن اصطحاب الأطفال؟
hal min-nal mum-kin is-ti-haa-bul at-faal?

Do you have...? | هل عندك...؟
hal 'in-da-ka...?

a high chair | كرسي أطفال
kur-si' atfal

a cot | مهد
mahd

> **Doctor** (p 126)

Reference

Measurements and quantities

Liquids السوائل as-sa-waa-il

half a litre of...	نصف لتر	nisf li-tir...
one litre of...	لتر واحد	li-tar waa-hid...
two litres of...	لتران	lit-raan...
a carafe/jug of...	دورق	daw-raq...
a bottle of...	قنينة	qin-nii-nah...
a glass of...	زجاج	zu-jaa-ja...

Weights الأوزان al-aw-zaan

100 grams of...	١٠٠ غرام	100 qa-raam...
half a kilo of...	نصف كيلو	nisf kii-loo...
one kilo of...	كيلو واحد	kii-loo waa-hid...
two kilos of...	كيلوان	kii-loo-waan...

Food الغذاء al-qi-thaa

a slice of...	شريحة	sha-rii-ha...
a portion of...	جزء	juz...
a dozen	دزينة	du-zee-na...
a box/tin of...	صندوق/علبة	sun-duuq/'ul-ba...
a carton of...	كارتون	kar-toon...
a packet of...	حزمة	hiz-ma...
a jar of...	جرة	jar-ra...

Numbers

In Arabic, numbers are followed by the singular, so you would ask for six peach, two tea, seven stamp, etc.

٠	**0**	صفر	sifr
١	**1**	واحد	waa-hid
٢	**2**	إثنان	ith-naan
٣	**3**	ثلاثة	tha-laa-tha
٤	**4**	أربعة	ar-ba-'a
٥	**5**	خمسة	kham-sa
٦	**6**	ستة	sit-ta
٧	**7**	سبعة	sab-'a
٨	**8**	ثمانية	tha-maa-ni-ya

٩	**9**	تسعة	tis-'a
١٠	**10**	عشرة	'a-sha-ra
١١	**11**	أحد عشر	a-ha-da 'a-shar
١٢	**12**	إثنا عشر	ith-naa 'a-shar
١٣	**13**	ثلاثة عشر	tha-laa-tha 'a-shar
١٤	**14**	أربعة عشر	ar-ba-'a-ta 'a-shar
١٥	**15**	خمسة عشر	kham-sa-ta 'a- shar
١٦	**16**	ستة عشر	sit-ta-ta 'a-shar
١٧	**17**	سبعة عشر	sab-'a-ta 'a-shar
١٨	**18**	ثمانية عشر	tha-maa-niya-ta 'a-shar
١٩	**19**	تسعة عشر	tis-'a-ta 'a-shar
٢٠	**20**	عشرون	'ish-ruun
٢١	**21**	واحد و عشرون	waa-hid wa 'ish-ruun
٢٢	**22**	إثنان وعشرون	ith-naan wa 'ish-ruun
٣٠	**30**	ثلاثون	tha-laa-thuun
٤٠	**40**	أربعون	ar-ba-'uun
٥٠	**50**	خمسون	kham-suun
٦٠	**60**	ستون	sit-tuun
٧٠	**70**	سبعون	sab-'uun
٨٠	**80**	ثمانون	tha-maa-nuun
٩٠	**90**	تسعون	tis-'uun
١٠٠	**100**	مائة	mi-ah
٢٠٠	**200**	مئتان	mi-a-taan
٣٠٠	**300**	ثلاث مائة	tha-laa-thu mi-ah
٤٠٠	**400**	أربع مائة	ar-ba-u mi-ah
٥٠٠	**500**	خمس مائة	kham-su mi-ah

١،٠٠٠	**1,000**	ألف	alf
٢،٠٠٠	**2,000**	ألفان	al-faan
٣،٠٠٠	**3,000**	ثلاث آلاف	tha-laa-thu aa-laaf
١٠،٠٠٠	**10,000**	عشرة آلاف	ash-ra-tu aa-laaf
١٠٠،٠٠٠	**100,000**	مائة ألف	mi-a-tu alf
١،٠٠٠،٠٠٠	**1,000,000**	مليون	mil-yoon

first	الأول	al-aw-wal
second	الثاني	ath-thaa-nii
third	الثالث	ath-thaa-lith
fourth	الرابع	ar-raa-bi
fifth	الخامس	al-khaa-mis
sixth	السادس	as-saa-dis
seventh	السابع	as-saa-bi'
eighth	الثامن	ath-thaa-min
ninth	التاسع	at-taa-si'
tenth	العاشر	al-'aa-shir

Days and months

Days

Monday	الإثنين	al-ith-nain
Tuesday	الثلاثاء	ath-thu-laa-thaa
Wednesday	الأربعاء	al-ar-bi-'aa
Thursday	الخميس	al-kha-miis
Friday	الجمعة	al-jum-'a
Saturday	السّبت	as-sabt
Sunday	الأحد	al-a-had

Months

January	يناير/كانون الثّاني	ya-naa-yir/kaa-nuun ath-thaa-nii
February	فبراير/شباط	fib-raa-yir/shi-baat
March	مارس/آذار	maa-ris/aa-thaar
April	أبريل/نيسان	ab-riil/nii-saan
May	مايو/أيار	maa-yoo
June	يونيو/حزيران	yuun-yuu/ hu-zay-raan
July	يوليو/تموز	yuul-yuu/ta-muuz
August	أغسطس/آب	a-qus-tus/aab
September	سبتمبر/أيلول	sib-tam-bar/ay-luul

Days and months

October	أكتوبر/تشرين الأول	ak-too-ber/tish-riin al-aw-wal
November	نوفمبر/تشرين الثّاني	noo-fam-ber/ tish-riin ath-thaa-nii
December	ديسمبر/كانون الأول	dii-sam-ber/ kaa-nuun al-aw-wal

Seasons

spring	الربيع	ar-ra-bii'
summer	الصيف	as-sayf
autumn	الخريف	al-kha-riif
winter	الشتاء	ash-shi-taa

Time

The 24-hour clock is used on timetables, etc.

am (morning) صباحا
sa-baa-han

It's midday الظهر
ath-thuhr

pm (afternoon)	مساءا ma-saa-an
It's...	انها in-na-haa
It's one o'clock	انها الساعة الواحدة in-na-haa as-saa-'ah al waa-hi-da
It's two o'clock	انها الساعة الثانية in-na-haa as-saa-'ah ath-thaa-ni-ya
What time is it?	كم الساعة؟ kamis-saa-'ah?

الساعة التاسعة as-saa-'atut-taa-si-'a	9.00
الساعة التاسعة و عشر دقائق as-saa-'atut-taa-si-'a wa 'ash-ru da-qaa-iq	9.10

الساعة التاسعة و خمسة عشر دقيقة as-saa-'atut-taa-si-'a wa kham-sa-ta 'ash-ra da-qii-qa	quarter past nine
الساعة التاسعة و نصف as-saa-'atut-taa-si-'a wa nisf	9.30
الساعة العاشرة إلا ربع as-saa-'atul-'aa-shi-rah il-laa rub'	quarter to ten
الساعة العاشرة إلا عشر دقائق as-saa-'atul-'aa-shi-rah il-laa 'ash-ru da-qaa-iq	9:50

What is the date? ما التاريخ؟
mat-taa-riikh?

It's the 16th September 2007 إنه السادس عشر من سبتمبر/أيلول ٢٠٠٧
in-na-hu as-saa-di-sa 'a-sh-r min sib-tam-bar/ay-luul 2007

today	اليوم al-yawm
tomorrow	غدا qa-dan
yesterday	أمس ams

Time phrases

When does it begin?	متى يبدأ؟ ma-taa yab-da?
When does it finish?	متى ينتهي؟ ma-taa yan-ta-hii?
When does it open?	متى يفتح؟ ma-taa yaf-tah?
When does it close?	متى يغلق؟ ma-taa yuq-liq?

When does it leave?	متى يغادر؟ ma-taa yu-qaa-dir?
When does it return?	متى يعود؟ ma-taa ya-'uud?
at 3 o'clock	في السّاعة الثّالثة fis-saa-'a-tith-thaa-li-tha
before 3 o'clock	قبل السّاعة الثّالثة qab-la as-saa-'a ath-thaa-li-tha
after 3 o'clock	بعد السّاعة الثّالثة ba'-da as-saa-'a ath-thaa-li-tha
in the morning	في الصباح fis-sa-baah
this morning	هذا الصباح haa-thas-sa-baah
in the afternoon (until dusk)	بعد الظهر ba'-dath-thuhr

in the evening (after dusk)	في المساء fil-ma-saa
in an hour's time	خلال مدّة ساعة khi-laa-la saa-'ah

Eating out

Eating places

كشك kushk
Snack bar or street stall that sells sandwiches and pastries

دكان الكباب dukan al kabab
Small kebab shop

مخبز makhbaz
Serves pitta bread with a variety of toppings. Arabic equivalent of a pizzeria

محل الكعك و الحلويات mahal ka'ak wa hul wiyat
Cake shop that serves cakes, pastries and soft drinks

مطعم mat'am

Licensed restaurant with waiter service. Although lunch is normally served from 12 to 2 pm and dinner from 7 to 10 pm, restaurants in Turkey will usually serve food outside these times as well

كافتريا cafteria

Serves a selection of ready-prepared dishes

In a café

FACE TO FACE

A ماذا تحب؟

maa-thaa tu-hib?

What would you like?

B شاي بالحليب رجاءا

shaay bil ha-liib ra-jaa-an

A tea with milk please

A ... please	رجاءً ... ...ra-jaa-an
two ... please	٢ ... رجاءً 2 ... ra-jaa-an
three ... please	٣ ... رجاءً 3 ... ra-jaa-an
Do you have...?	هل عندك ...؟ hal 'in-da-ka...?
Do you have coffee?	هل عندك قهوة؟ hal 'in-da-ka qah-wa?
Do you have orange juice?	هل عندك عصير برتقال؟ hal 'in-da-ka as ir bur tu kal?
A bottle of sparkling water	قنينة من الماء الفوّار qin-nii-na min al-maa al-faw-waar
sparkling (water)	الماء الفوّار al-maa al-faw-waar
mineral (still water)	ماء معدني (ماء عادي) maa ma'-da-ni (maa 'aadi)

A cappuccino, please	كابتشينو، رجاء kabat-chii-noo, ra-jaa-an
A tea, please	شاي ، رجاء shaay, ra-jaa-an
with milk	بالحليب bil-ha-liib
with lemon	بالليمون bil-lay-muun
with ice	بالثلج bith-thalj
with sugar	بالسكّر bis-suk-kar
without sugar	بدون سكّر bi-duun suk-kar
one more, please	واحد آخر، رجاء waa-hid aa-khar, ra-jaa-an

In a restaurant

You will never be stuck for somewhere to eat in most Arab countries. There are eating places everywhere, and they are usually open from early in the morning until late at night. If you were planning to eat a full meal, you would begin with مقبلات mu-qab-bilaat (starter), followed by الوجبة الرئيسية al-waj-bah ar-ra-ii-siy-yah (main course), and end with حلوى hal-waa (dessert), or just tea or coffee. Dinner is a very sociable occasion: people often sit and talk for hours.

Food is mostly served warm rather than hot, with the exception of soup.

Is there a good restaurant?	هل هناك مطعم جيد؟ hal hu-naa-ka mat-'am jay-yid?
The menu, please	القائمة، رجاء al-qaa-i-ma, ra-jaa-an
Is there a set menu?	هل هناك قائمة طعام؟ hal hu-naa-ka qaa-i-ma-tu ta-'aam?

What is this?	ما هذا؟ maa haa-thaa?
I'd like this	أنا أريد هذا anaa u-rii-du haa-thaa
What is the speciality of the house?	ما اختصاص المطعم؟ maa ikh-ti-saa-sul mat'am?
with chips	بالبطاطس bil-ba-taa-tis
with salad	بالسلطة bis-sa-la-da
no onion, please	بدون بصل، رجاء bi-duun ba-sal, ra-jaa-an
no tomatoes, please	بدون طماطم، رجاء bi-duun ta-maa-tim, ra-jaa-an
Excuse me!	لو سمحت! law sa-mah-t!
The bill, please	الحساب، لو سمحت al-hi-saab, law sa-mah-t

Some more bread, please	مزيدا من الخبز، رجاءً ma-zii-dan minal-khubz, ra-jaa-an
Some more water, please	مزيدا من الماء، رجاءً ma-zii-dan minal al-maa, ra-jaa-an
salt	الملح al-mil-h
pepper	الفلفل al-fil-fil
Another bottle, please	زجاجة اخرى، رجاء zu-jaa-ja-tun u-kh-raa, ra-jaa-an
Another glass, please	كأس اخر، رجاء ka-sun aa-khar, ra-jaa-an

Vegetarian

There are no specialist vegetarian restaurants. In any restaurant, however, there are vegetarian dishes available.

I am vegetarian	أنا نباتيّ anaa na-baa-ti
I don't eat meat	أنا لا آكُلُ لحمَ anaa laa aa-ku-lul-lahma
Is there meat in this?	هَلْ هناك لحم في هذا؟ hal hu-naa-ka lahm fii haa-thaa?
What is there without meat?	هل هناك شيء بدون لحمٍ؟ hal hu-naa-ka she-y bi-duun lahm?

Wines and spirits

Alcohol is forbidden by Islam, although some Arabs drink. In some Arab countries, the possession of alcohol is strictly forbidden to everyone. In other countries, like Iraq, it is legal and available to foreigners.

The wine list, please	قائمة الخمر، رجاءً qaa-i-ma-tul- kham-ri, ra-jaa-an
Can you recommend a good wine?	هَلّ بالإمكان أنْ تَنصحني بخمر جيد؟ hal bil-im-kaa-ni an tan-sah-nii bi kham-rin jay-yid?
A bottle of...	زجاجة من... zu-jaa-jah min...
red wine	خمر أحمر kham-r ah-mar

Eating out

rosé wine	خمر وردي kham-r war-di
white wine	خمر أبيض kham-r ab-yad
A glass of...	كأس من... ka-s min...
a dry wine	خمر جاف kham-r jaaf
a local wine	خمر محلي kham-r ma-hal-lii
a sweet wine	خمر حلو kham-r hil-w
What liqueurs do you have?	أي الخمور عندك؟ ay-yul khu-muu-ri 'in-dak?

Menu reader

Below are some dishes from different countries. Names of dishes are written in the local dialect of each country which might be different from the classical Arabic.

Egypt

aish عيش
bread

asab عصاب
sugar cane juice

ayesh beladi عيش بلدي
flat pitta bread made with wholemeal flour

ayesh shami عيش شامي
flat pitta bread made with white flour

baba ghanoush بابا غنوش
baked aubergine ground with tahini (paste made from seasme seeds), spices and garlic

baklawa بقلاوة
a baked pastry made of layers of filo dough and nuts and covered with syrup

bamia بامية
meat and okra stew

basal akhdar بصل أخضر
green onions

basboosa بسبوسة
semolina cake with honey-lemon syrup

bastermah (or **basterma**) بسطرمة
dried cured beef

batarekh بتاركه
salted and dried fish roe

batt baladi بط بلدي
duck

beid hhamine بيض حامين
Egyptian slow-cooked eggs

belah بلح
dates

besara بصارة
mashed broad beans made into a purée and cooked

biram ruzz بيرام رز
baked rice with chicken

couscous كسكس
a dish based on savoury semolina that can be combined with egg, chicken, lamb or vegetables

esh es seraya عيش السرايا
sweet made with bread and honey

falafel فلافل
blend of broad beans, parsley, garlic and herbs, shaped into patties and deep-fried

fegl فجل
radish

feteer meshaltet فطير مشلت
Egyptian puff pastry with dips

fireek فريك
toasted wheat

fiteer فطير
round pastry made with layers of filo dough and butter

fool akhdar فول أخضر
fresh green broad beans, eaten with white cheese

fool medames فول مدمس
broad bean stew

fool nabet فول نابت
broad bean soup

fool nabit
sprouted broad beans

gargeer جرجير
watercress

gargir جارجير
Egyptian rocket

gebnah areesh جبنة عريش
white cheese

gibna beida جبنة بيضاء
feta-style cheese

gibna rumy جبنة رومي
cheddar-style cheese

guafa جوافة
guava

hamam mahshi حمام محشي
pigeons stuffed with bulgur wheat

hammem حمام
pigeon

hummus حمص
chickpeas puréed with tahini and lemon and served as a dip

hummus bi tahini حمص بالطحينة
chickpea and sesame dip

irk sous عرق سوس
liquorice root drink

korrat كرات
leeks

koshari كشري
red lentils and rice

kuftat كفتة
spiced meatballs

kunafa كنافة
baked pastry made of layers of shredded wheat dough and nuts and covered with syrup

lebb لب
roasted watermelon seeds

lebb abyad لب أبيض
roasted pumpkin seeds

lebb suri لب سوري
roasted sunflower seeds

maashi محشي
stuffed vegetables

mekhalel مخلل
pickles

malana ملانا
green chickpea shoots

meshmesheyya مشمشية
dried apricots

mihallabiya مهلبية
rose-scented pudding

milookhiyya (molokheyya) ملوخية
green herb soup

mish ميش
fermented cheese

mulukhiyyah ملوخية
spinach-like vegetable

oom ali أم علي
warm dessert consisting of a pudding with raisins and coconut and a cereal topping

qahwa قهوة
coffee

romann رمان
pomegranate

roz bel laban رز باللبن
rice and milk

sardeen memalla سردين مملح
salted sardines

sasal eswed عسل أسود
molasses

seish baladi عيش بلدي
bread made of whole wheat flour

seish dorah عيش درة
bread made from corn flour

seish saymeen عيش صايمين
fasting people's bread

seish shami عيش شامي
pitta bread

sudani سوداني
peanuts

tahini طحينة
sesame seed paste. Often served mildly spiced with lemon, garlic, salt and pepper as a dip for bread

tammeya تمية
fried vegetable patty made of ground broad beans (fool) and spices

taratour طرطور
sesame sauce

teen تين
figs

teen shoki تين شوكي
prickly pear

toot توت
mulberry fruit. There are two types, red and white.

torshi ترشي
pickled vegetables.

umm ali أم علي
pastry with milk, sugar and raisins

Morocco

amalou عمالو
argan oil, almond paste and honey spread

eghrir الغرير
Moroccan pancakes

bistteeya, basteela, or pastilla بستية
puffed pastry stuffed with chicken, eggs and almonds baked and covered with powdered sugar and cinnamon

brik bil lahm بريك باللحم
lamb turnover

briouat بريوات
stuffed pastry triangle

briouat bel Kofta بريوات بالكفتة
stuffed pastry triangle with minced meat and spices

chabakiya شبكية
Moroccan sweet

charmoula (chermoula) شرمولة
tangy sauce made from cumin, lemon juice, salt, black pepper, sweet paprika, ginger, marjoram, and olive oil

chakchouka شكشوكة
peppers, garlic, cumin and tomatoes cooked with harissa and olive oil, with eggs

chroba fassia شربة فاسية
vegetable soup, originally from Fez city

couscous كسكسو
a dish based on savoury semolina that can be combined with egg, chicken, lamb or vegetables

dejaj laimoun دجاج ليمون
chicken with lemons

djej emshmel دجاج مشمل
roasted chicken cooked with olives and lemon

djej bil einab دجاج بالعنب
chicken with grapes

djej Kdra Touimiya دجاج كدرا طعمية
chicken with almonds and chickpeas

djaja mahamara دجاجة محمرة
chicken stuffed with almonds, semolina and raisins

djeja M'Qalli دجاج مقلي
chicken with coriander & mint

feqqas فقاس
biscuits with aniseed and orange blossom

ferakh maamer فراخ معمر
spring chicken with couscous stuffing

ghoriba غريبة
biscuits covered in almonds or sesame seeds

halwa shebakia حلوى شبكية
sesame biscuits eaten during Ramadan

harcha حرشة
semolina pancakes

harira حريرة
vegetable soup with lamb, lentils, tomatoes, chickpeas and spices. National soup of Morocco, cooked during Ramadan

harissa هريسة
garlic, chilli, salt and olive oil paste usually served with couscous

hout حوت
fish stew

kaab-el-ghzal كعب الغزال
('gazelle's horns') pastry stuffed with almond paste and topped with sugar

kamfounata كمفوناتة
Moroccan ratatouille

kamoun كمون
cumin

kasbour كزبر
coriander

kefta كفته
meatballs

kharkoum كركم
turmeric

kisra or **khboz** كسرة أو خبز
leavened bread flavoured with aniseed

khboz bishemar خبز بشمار
Marrakesh 'pizza'

khubz araby خبز عربي
pocket bread

kouclas bi khobz ككلاس بالخبز
bread dumplings

kouclas bi ruz ككلاس بالرز
rice dumplings

haloua tpolo حلاوة تبولو
chocolate-sesame cones

hut b'Noua حوت بالنوة
fish with almond paste

hut bu-Etob حوت بالبلح
fish stuffed with dates

lahm el Mahammer لحم محمر
lamb in a red sauce

Lahm Maqli لحم مقلي
lamb with olives and lemons

lahm Mashwi لحم مشوي
lamb kebabs

leben لبن
popular milk drink

libzar لبزار
pepper

maadnous معدنوس
parsley

matbucha مطبوشة
pepper and tomato salad

mahancha محنشة
thin pastry filled with almonds

m'semmen مسمن
pancacke served with honey or sugar

mechoui مشوي
roasted lamb

m'hanncha محنشة
(the snake) coiled almond pastry

mourouzia (mzouria) مروزية
sweet lamb dish with raisins, almonds and honey

mslalla مسللى
marinated olives

qamama كمامة
lamb tajine with honey and onions

qubdan كبد
spiced lamb kebabs

ras-el-hanout رأس الحانوت
classic blend of spices

rayib رايب
yoghurt with artichoke hearts

righaif رغاف
pancake with honey and sesame seeds

sfinj سفنج
doughnuts

skingbir سكنجبير
ginger

seffa سفة
couscous sprinkled with almonds, cinnamon and sugar

sharbat شربات
apple milk drink

shabbakia شبكية
small cakes fried in oil and coated with honey

shlada bi lichine شلدا باللشين
orange and walnut salad

smen سمن
butter based cooking oil

tagine طاجن
lamb or chicken stew cooked in an earthenware pot with vegetables, almonds and plums. If made with fish it is called **hout**

tagine barrogog bis basela طجين برقوق بسبسلا
lamb tajine with prunes

tfaia تفايا
lamb tajine with eggs and almonds

warkha ورقة
thin pastry sheets

zaafrane beldi زعفران بلدي
saffron

zalouk زلوك
salad with aubergines

Tunisia

....

brik بريك
triangular shaped envelope of crispy pastry containing a lightly cooked egg topped with fresh herbs and tuna

boukha بوخة
fig brandy

brik à l'oeuf بريك بالبيض
triangular envelope of crispy pastry containing a whole egg and a filling

chakchouka شكشوكة
type of ratatouille with peppers, tomatoes and egg

couscous كسكسي
Tunisia's national dish, served with vegetables, lamb, poultry or fish

chorba' شربة
thick soup made with tomatoes, onions and pasta

coucha كوشة
shoulder of lamb cooked with Cayenne pepper and turmeric

felfel mahchi فلفل محشي
peppers stuffed with meat and served with harissa sauce

guenaoia قناوية (باميا)
lamb or beef stew with chillies, okra, sweet peppers and coriander

harissa هريسة
garlic, chilli, salt and olive oil paste usually served with couscous

koucha fil kolla كوشة في القلة

fresh lamb sprinkled with rosemary and spices and baked in a clay pot

koucha bil aallouch كوشة بالعلوش

shoulder of lamb with potato

halim (halalim) حلالم

noodle soup

lalabli لبلابي

garlic and chickpea soup

makroudh مقروض

syrup-soaked honey cake stuffed with dates

mechouia سلاطة مشوية

salad of grilled sweet peppers, tomatoes and onions mixed with olive oil and lemon, tuna fish and hard-boiled eggs

mhalbya محلبية

cake made with rice, nuts and geranium water

merguez مرقاز

small spicy sausages

mloukhia (mloukhiya) ملوخية

beef or lamb stew with bay leaves

Ojja عجة

scrambled eggs mixed with tomatoes, pimentos, peppers and garlic

osben عصبان
type of sausage

salata batata سلاطة بطاطا
hot potato salad with caraway seeds

samsa صمصة
almond and sesame pastries

shorba frik شربة فريك
lamb soup with tomato paste, coriander and parsley, served with slices of lemon

michwiya سلاطة مشوية
salad made with grilled tomatoes, peppers and onions

tagine طاجين
lamb or chicken stew cooked in an earthenware pot with vegetables, almonds and plums

torshi طرشي
pickled turnips

thibarine تيبارين
Tunisian date liquor

yo-yo يويو
doughnuts made with orange juice, deep fried then dipped in honey syrup

Grammar

Arabic grammar is often found to be difficult and complicated. Like most languages, it adheres to grammatical rules. Below are some important features of Arabic grammar.

Article

The article **'al-'** expresses the definite state of a noun of any gender and number.

Grammatical cases

Arabic has three grammatical cases roughly corresponding to: nominative, genitive and accusative, and three numbers: singular, dual and plural.

Normally, nouns take the ending -**u(n)** in the nominative, -**i(n)** in the genitive and -**a(n)** in the accusative. However, with important exceptions, case is not shown in standard orthography, and it is optional whether to articulate a case ending when speaking or reading aloud.

The plural of a noun is formed by a suffix in some cases **(sound plurals)**, but frequently, the vowel structure of a word is changed to form the plural **(broken plurals)**. There are a number of patterns to how this is done. Some singular nouns take several plurals. The plurals of nouns representing humans usually use sound plurals. Masculine sound plurals take the forms **'–ūn'** in the nominative and **'–īn'** in the genitive and accusative. In the feminine, the ending is **'–āt'** and is limited in its declension to two forms: one for the nominative, and another for both other cases. For example, **'–ātun'** and **'–ātin'** are possible, but not **'–ātan'**. This pattern can also be used for plurals of non-human nouns.

Genders

Arabic has two genders, expressed by pronominal, verbal and adjectival agreement. Agreement with numerals shows a peculiar 'polarity'. The genders are usually referred to as masculine and feminine.

Verbs

As in many other Semitic languages, Arabic verb formation is based on a (usually) triconsonantal root, which is not a word in itself but contains the semantic core. The consonants **k-t-b**, for example, indicate 'write', **q-r-a** indicate 'read', **a-k-l** indicate 'eat', etc. Words are formed by supplying the root with a vowel structure and with affixes.

Personal pronouns

Person	Singular	Plural	Dual
3rd (m) he/they	huwa	hum	humā
3rd (f) she/they	hiya	hunna	hunna
2nd (m) you	anta	antum	antumā
2nd (f) you	anti	antunna	antunna
1st I	ana	nahnu	(n/a)

Attached pronouns

Enclitic forms of the pronoun may be affixed to nouns (representing genitive case, for example, possession) and to verbs (representing accusative, for example, a direct object). Most of them are clearly related to the full personal pronouns. They are identical in form in both cases, except for the first person singular, which is **-ī** after nouns (genitive) and **-nī** after verbs (accusative).

Person	Singular	Plural	Dual
3rd (m) him/them	-hu	-hum	-humā
3rd (f) her/them	-hā	-hunna	-hunna
2nd (m) you	-ka	-kum	-kumā
2nd (f) you	-ki	-kunna	-kunna
1st me/us	-(n)ī/-ya	-nā	(n/a)

Public holidays

There are two major Islamic religious holidays, called '**Eid al-Fitr**' and '**Eid al-Adhaa**', each lasting two to three days. They are determined by the lunar calendar, so their dates vary from year to year. The first one is the Feast of Ramadan, which marks the end of the holy month of Ramadan. The second is the Feast of Sacrifice; the most important holiday of the year, which marks the end of the Hadj (pilgrimage) of millions of Muslims to the Holylands of Saudi Arabia.

Signs and notices

Most signs in airports and stations are bilingual. Most shops and restaurants in big cities and tourist-orientated places have English information boards as well as Arabic ones.

At the station

المحطة	al-ma-had-da	station
المترو	al-mit-ro	metro
خروج	khu-ruuj	exit
البوابة الغربية	al-baw-waa-bah al-qar-biy-yah	west gate
البوابة الشمالية	al-baw-waa-bah ash-sha-maa-li-ya	north gate
مخرج الطوارئ	makh-raj at-ta-waa-ri	emergency exit
التذكرة	at-that-ka-ra	ticket
جواز السفر	ja-waaz as-sa-far	passport

كوبونات	ko-boo-naat	voucher/coupon
قسم المبيعات	qism al-ma-bii-'aat	sales section
الخطوط المحليّة	al-khu-tuut al-jaw-wiy-yah	local lines
أطفال	at-faal	children
بالغ	baa-liq	adult
درهم	dir-ham	dirham

Inside the station

الرصيف	ar-ra-siif	platform
المصعد	al-mis-'ad	lift
دِرج	da-raj	stairs
كرسي المعوقين	kur-si al-mu-' aw-wa-qiin	wheelchair
صعود	su-'uud	going up
هبوط	hu-buut	going down

Vending machine/telephone

ماء	maa'	water
شاي عربي	sha-y 'a-ra-bi	Arabic tea
صراف	sar-raaf	money exchange
نفذ	na-fath	out of stock
عاطل	aa-til	out of order
فكة	fak-ka	change
كشك	kush-k	kiosk
هاتف	haa-tif	telephone
دولي	du-wali	international
محلي	ma-hal-li	national
بطاقة	bi-taa-qa	card
ادفع	id-fa	push
اسحب	is-hab	pull

In the bus

مفتوح	maf-tuuh	open
مغلق	muq-laq	close
ممنوع التدخين	mam-nuu' at-tad-khiin	non-smoking
للتدخين	lit-tad-khiin	smoking

مرحاض	mir-haad	toilet
نساء	ni-saa	women
رجال	ri-jaal	men

On the street (places and related words)

مصرف/ بنك	mis-raf	bank
صيدلية	say-da-liy-yah	pharmacy
فندق	fun-duq	hotel
مطعم	mat-'am	restaurant
مقهى	maq-haa	coffee shop
مغسلة بخارية	maq-sala bu-khaa-riy-yah	dry-cleaner's
السوق المركزي	as-suuq al-mar-ka-zi	supermarket
مركز الشرطة	mar-kaz ash-shurta	police station
غرف متوفرة	qu-raf mu-ta-waf-fira	room available
لا توجد غرف شاغرة	laa tuu-jad quraf shaa-qira	no vacancies
الدكان مفتوح	ad-duk-kaan maftuuh	shop is open

الدكان مغلق	ad-duk-kaan muq-laq	shop is closed
الطوارئ	at-ta-waa-ri	emergency

On the street (other road signs)

خطر	kha-tar	danger
توقّف	ta-waq-qaf	stop
اعبر	u'-bur	cross
تحت الإنشاءات	tah-tal inshaa	under construction
ممنوع	mam-nuu'	prohibited
منعطف الى اليمين	mun-'a-taf ilal-ya-miin	right turning
منعطف الى اليسار	mun-'a-taf ilal-ya-saar	left turning
إلى الأمام	ilal-amaam	straight on
طريق المشاة	ta-riiqul-mushaa	pedestrian path
دراجة	dar-raa-jah	bicycle
سيارة	say-yaa-rah	automobile
مشاة	mu-shaa	pedestrians
جسر المشاة	jisrul-mushaa	pedestrian bridge
إشارة مرور	ishaa-rat mu-ruur	traffic signal

Outside the station/taxi stand

موقف	maw-qif	parking
حافلة	haa-fila	bus
سيارة أجرة	say-yaa-rat uj-ra	taxi
سيارة صغيرة	say-yaa-ra sa-qii-ra	small vehicle
سيارة كبيرة	say-yaa-ra ka-bii-ra	large vehicle
السيارات متوفرة	as-say-yaa-raat mu-ta-wa-fi-ra	cars available

At the restaurant/shop

الفطور	al-fu-tuur	breakfast
الغداء	al-qa-daa	lunch
العشاء	al-'a-shaa	dinner
وجبات الطعام التقليدية	wa-ja-baat at-ta-'aam at-taq-lii-diya	traditional meals
وجبات الطعام الغربية	wa-ja-baat at-ta-'aam al-qar-biy-ya	western meals

الضريبة	ad-da-rii-ba	tax
متضمّن للضريبة ورسم الخدمة	mu-ta-dam-min lid-da-rii-ba wa rasm al-khid-ma	tax and service charge included
غير متضمّن للضريبة ورسم الخدمة خاصّة	qayr mu-ta-dam-min lid-da-rii-ba wa rasm al-khid-ma	tax and service charge not included
المشروبات	al-mash-ruu-baat	drinks

English – Arabic

A

a (n)		
about	حول	hawl
above	فوق	fawqa
to accept	قبل	qabila
accident	حادث	haadith
ache: it aches	وجع: يوجّع	waja': yuuji'
address	عنوان	'in-waan
admission charge	قيمة الدخول	qiimat addukhuul
adult	بالغ	baaliq
aeroplane	طائرة	taa-irah
after	بعد	ba'd
afternoon	العصر	al-'asr
this afternoon	بعد ظهر اليوم	ba'da thuhril-yawm
in the afternoon	بعد الظهر	ba'dath-thuhr
tomorrow afternoon	بعد ظهر الغد	ba'da thuhril-qad
again	ثانية	thaaniyatan
age	العمر	al-'umr
agent	الوكيل	al-wakiil
estate agent	وكيل العقارات	wakiil al-'aqa araat
travel agent	وكيل السفريات	wakiil as-safariyaat
ago	مضى	mathaa
ahead: straight ahead	للأمام: مباشرة للأمام	lil-amaam: mubaasharatan lil-amaam
air conditioning	التكييف	at-takyiif
airport	مطار	mataar
alarm	جرس الإنذار	jaras al-inthaar

alarm clock	الساعة المنبهة	as-saa'atul munab-bih
alcohol	الكحول	al-kuhuul
without alcohol	بدون كحول	bidoon kuhuul
all	الكل	al-kul
to be allergic to	حساسية من	hasaa-siyah min
all right (ok)	حسنا	hasanan
alone	وحيد	wahiid
always	دائما	daa-iman
ambulance	سيارة الإسعاف	sayyaarat is'aaf
America	أمريكا	amriikaa
American	الأمريكي	al-amriikii
and	و	wa
angry	غاضب	qaadib
another	آخر	aakhar
another beer	بيرة أخرى	biira ukhraa

answer	جواب	jawaab
there's no answer (phone)	ليس هناك جواب (هاتف)	laysa hunaaka jawaab (haatif)
to answer	أجاب	ajaaba
answering machine	جهاز الإجابة الآلي	ji-haaz al ija ba al aali
ants	النمل	an-naml
any: have you any matches?	أي: هل لديك أي كبريت؟	ayyu: hal ladayka ayyu kibriit?
apartment	شقة	shuqqah
apple	تفاح	tuffaah
apple juice	عصير التفاح	asiir at-tufaa
April	أبريل/نيسان	abriil/niisaan
arm	ذراع	thiraa'
my arm hurts	ذراعي يؤلمني	thiraa'ii yu-thiinii
to arrest	إعتقل	i'taqala
arrivals	القادمون	al-qaadimuun

to arrive	وصل	wasala
art gallery	المعرض الفني	al-ma'rad al-fanni
artist	فنان	fannaan
ashtray	منفضة السجائر	minfathat as-sajaa-ir
asthma	الربو	ar-rabuu
at	في	fii
to attack	هاجم	haajama
attack	هجوم	hujuum
heart attack	النوبة القلبية	an-nawba al-qalbiyyah
attention	إنتباه	intibaah
attractive	جذّاب	jath-thaab
August	أغسطس/آب	aqustus/aab
aunt	عمّة	'ammah
Australia	أستراليا	usturaaliyaa
Australian	أسترالي	usturaalii
automatic car	سيارة أتوماتيك	sayyaarah otto-matiik
autumn	خريف	khariif
away: please go away!	بعيدا: رجاء إبعد عني!	ba'iidan: rajaa-an ib'id 'annii!

B

baby	الطفل الرضيع	at-tiflur-radii'
baby food	غذاء طفل رضيع	qidaa tifl radii'
babysitter	جليسة الأطفال	raa'iyat al atfaal
back (of body)	ظهر (من الجسم)	thahr (min al-jism)
backpack	حقيبة الظهر	haqiibat ath-thahr
bad	سيئ	say-yi
bag	حقيبة	haqiiba
baggage	حقيبة	haqiiba
baggage reclaim	استرداد الحقائب	istirdaad al-haqaa-ib

English	Arabic	Pronunciation
baker's	خباز	khabaaz
ball	كرة	kurah
bandage	ضماد	dammaad
bank	مصرف	masraf
bar	حانة	haana
barber	حلاق	hallaaq
bargain	صفقة	safqah
no bargaining	لا مساومة	laa musaawamah
basket	سلة	sallaah
bath	حمّام	hammaam
bathroom	حمّام	hammaam
with bathroom	مع حمّام	bil-hammaam
battery (for car)	بطارية (للسيارة)	bat-taa-riya (lis-sayaarah)
the battery is flat	إنّ البطارية فارغة	innal-battaariya faariqah
bazaar	سوق	suuq
be	يكون	yakuun
beach	شاطئ	shaati
beautiful	جميل	jamiil
bed	سرير	sariir
double bed	سرير مزدوج	sariir muzdawaj
twin beds	أسرة مزدوجة	asirrah muzdawajah
bedclothes	غطاء الفراش	qitaaul-firaash
bedroom	غرفة النوم	qurfatun-nawm
double bedroom	غرفة النوم المزدوج	qurfat an-nawm al-muzdawaj
single bedroom	غرفة النوم الفردية	qurfat an-nawm al-fardiyyah
bee	نحلة	nahlah
beef	لحم البقر	lahmul baqar
before	قبل ذلك	qabla thaalik
before 4 o'clock	قبل السّاعة الرابعة	qablas-saa'ah ar-raabi'ah

English – Arabic

before dinner	قبل العشاء	qablal-'ashaa
to begin	بدأ	bada-a
behind	وراء	waraa
to believe	يصدق	usadiq
belly-dancing	الرقص الشرقي	ar-raqs ash-sharqi
below	تحت	tahta
belt	حزام	hizaam
money belt	حزام المال	hizaamul-maal
seat belt	حزام الأمان	hizaamul-al aman
bend	إنحناء	inhinaa
beside (next to)	بجانب (بجانب)	bi-jaanib
best	الأفضل	al-afthal
better (than)	أفضل (من)	afthal (min)
bicycle	دراجة هوائية	darraajah hawa'ya
big	كبير	kabiir
bigger	أكبر	akbar
biggest	الأكبر	al-akbar
bill	فاتورة	faatuura
the bill, please	الفاتورة، رجاء	al-faatuura, rajaa-an
bin (for rubbish)	سلة (للقمامة)	salla (lil-qumaama)
bird	طير	tayr
birthday	عيد الميلاد	iidul-miilaad
happy birthday!	عيد ميلاد سعيد!	iid milaad sa'iid!
birthday card	بطاقة عيد ميلاد	bitaa-qat 'iid milaad
biscuits	بسكويت	baskuwayt
bit: a bit	قطعة: قليلا	qit'a: qaliilan
bite (insect, dog)	عضة (حشرة، كلب)	ad-dah (hasharah, kalb)

bitter (taste)	مر (طعم)	mur (ta'aam)
black	أسود	as-wad
blanket	بطانية	bataaniyyah
to bleed	نزف	nazafa
blind (person)	أعمى (شخص)	a'maa (shakhs)
blinds (on window)	ستائر (على النافذة)	sataa-ir ('alaan-naafitha)
blister	بثرة	bathrah
blocked	مسدود	masduud
blood	دمّ	dam
blood group	فصيلة الدم	fasiilatud-dam
blood pressure	ضغط الدمّ	daqdud-dam
blue	أزرق	azraq
boarding card	بطاقة الركوب	bitaaqat rukuub
boat	مركب	markab
boat trip	رحلة الباخرة	rihlat al-baakhirah
boiled (food)	مغلي (غذاء)	maqlii (qithaa)
bone	عظم	athm
book	كتاب	kitaab
to book	حجز	hajaza
booking	حجز	hajz
bookshop	مكتبة	maktabah
boots	جزم	jizam
bottle	قنينة	qin-niinah
a bottle of water	قنينة الماء	qinniinatu maa
bottle opener	فتّاحة قنينة	fattaahat qinniinah
box	صندوق	sunduuq
box office	شباك التذاكر	shubbaak at-tathaakir
boy	ولد	walad
boyfriend	صديق	sadiiq
brandy	براندي	braandii

English	Arabic	Pronunciation
bread	خبز	khubz
to break	كسر	kasara
to break down (car)	تعطلت (سيارة)	ta'attalat (sayyaarah)
breakfast	فطور	futuur
breakfast included	الفطور مشمول	alfutuur mashmuul
to breathe	تنفّس	tanafasa
bring	احضر	ah-thir
British	بريطاني	britaani
brochure	الدليل	ad-daliil
broken	مكسور	maksuur
broken down (car, machine)	تعطل (سيارة، ماكنة)	ta'addala (sayyaarah, maakinah)
brother	أخّ	akh
brown	أسمر	asmar
brush	فرشاة	furshaa
hairbrush	فرشاة الشعر	furshaatush-sha'r
toothbrush	فرشاة الأسنان	furshaatu asnaan
bucket	سطل	satl
bulb (light)	لمبة	lamba
bureau de change	مكتب الصرافة	maktab as-sarraafa
burglary: there's been a burglary	سرقة: هناك سرقة	sirqa: hunaaka sirqa
to burn	أحرق	ahraqa
burn	حرقة	hurqah
burnt: it's burnt	إحترق: هو إحترق	ihtaraqa: huwa ihtaraqa
business	تجارة	tijaara
bus station	محطة الحافلات	mahattat al-haafilaat
bus stop	موقف الحافلات	mawqif al-haafilaat

busy: I'm busy	مشغول: انا مشغول	mashquul: anaa mashquul
butcher's	الجزّار	al-jazzaar
butter	الزبدة	az-zubda
to buy	اشترى	ishtaraa
can I buy this?	هلّ بالإمكان أن أشتري هذا؟	hal bil imkaani an ashtarii haathaa?
by	بـ	bi
by bus	بحافلة	bil-haafilaa
by train	بالقطار	bil-qitaar

C

café	مقهى	maqhaa
cake	كعكة	ka'kah
cake shop	دكان الكعك	dukaan al-ka'k
to call (on phone)	إتّصل (على الهاتف)	it-tasala ('alaal-haatif)
camcorder	آلة تصوير الفيديو النقّالة	aalat taswiir alfidyo an-naqaala
camel	جمل	jamal
camera	آلة التصوير	aalat taswiir
can	يمكن أن	yumkin an
a can of oil	علبة زيت	ilbat zayt
cancel	إلغاء	ilqaa
candle	شمعة	sham'a
can opener	فتّاحة العلب	fat-taahat 'ilba
car	سيارة	sayyaarah
by car	بالسيارة	bis-yaarah
car park	موقف سيارات	mawqif sayyaaraat
car seat (for child)	مقعد سيارة (للطفل)	maq'ad sayyaarah (lil atfaal)
caravan	قافلة	qaafila
card	بطاقة	bitaaqa

cards (playing)	كروت (لعب)	kuruut (la'ib)
carpet (rug)	سجادة (بساط)	sajjaadah (bisaat)
carry	إحمل	ihmil
to cash	صرف	sarafa
cash	نقدا	naqdan
cash desk	نقطة الدفع	nuqtat ad-daf'
castle	قلعة	qal'ah
cat	قطّة	qit'ah
caution	حذر	hathir
cave	كهف	kahf
CD	قرص مدمج	qurs mudmaj
CD player	مشغل القرص المدمج	mushaqil alqurs almudmaj
cemetery	مقبرة	maqbara
central	مركزي	markazii
central station	المحطة المركزية	al-mahatta al-markaziyya
town centre	مركز البلدة	markaz al-balad

certificate	شهادة	shahaada
chain	سلسلة	silsilah
chair	كرسي	kursi
champagne	شمبانيا	shambanyaa
change (coins)	الباقي (عملات معدنية)	al-baaqii ('umlaat ma'daniyah)
keep the change	إحتفظ بالباقي	ihtafith bilbaaqii
to change (money)	صرف (نقود)	sarafa (nuquud)
changing room	غرفة التغير	qurfatut-taqyiir
charge (fee)	القيمة (أجر)	al-qiima
cheap	رخيص	rakhiis
to check in	حضر	hathara
cheers!	هتافات!	hitaafaat!
cheese	جبنة	jubna!
chemist's	صيدلي	saydali

night-duty chemist	الصيدلي الليلي	as-saydali al-layli
cheque	شيك	shiik
cheque book	دفتر الشيكات	daftar ash-shiikaat
traveller's cheques	شيكات المسافرين	shiikaat almusaafiriin
cherry	كرز	karaz
chest (of body)	صدر (من الجسم)	sadr (min al-jism)
chewing gum	علكة	ilkah
chickenpox	جديري الماء	judari al-maa
child	طفل	tifl
chips	رقائق البطاطس	raqaa-iq al-bataatis
chocolate	شوكولاته	shukulaatah
hot chocolate	شوكولاته ساخنة	shukulaatah shakhina
chop (meat)	قطعة (لحم)	qit'ah (lahm)
Christmas	عيد الميلاد	iidul-miilaad
church	كنيسة	kaniisa
cigar	سيجار	sijaar
cigarettes	سجائر	sajaa-ir
a packet of cigarettes	علبة سجائر	ulbat sajaa-ir
cinema	سينما	sinima
circus	سيرك	sirk
city	مدينة	madiinah
city centre	مركز المدينة	markaz al-madiinah
to clean	نظف	nath-thafa
clean	نظيف	nathiif
it's not clean	هو ليس نظيف	huwa laysa nathiif
climbing: to go climbing	التسلّق: الذهاب للتسلّق	at-tasalluq: ath-thahaab lit-tasalluq
cloakroom	حجرة المعاطف	hujrat al-ma'aatif

English	Arabic	Pronunciation
clock	ساعة	saa'ah
close: is it close by?	قريب: هل هو قريب؟	qariib: hal huwa qariib?
to close	أغلق	aqlaqa
when does it close?	متى يغلق؟	mataa yuqliqu?
closed	مغلق	muqlaq
is it closed?	هل هو مغلق؟	hal huwa muqlaq?
clothes	ملابس	malaabis
coast	ساحل	saahil
coat	معطف	mi'taf
cocoa	كاكاو	kaakaa-w
cockroach	صرصار	sursaar
coconut	جوز الهند	jawzul-hind
coffee	قهوة	qahwa
black coffee	قهوة سوداء	qahwa sawdaa
iced coffee	قهوة مبردة	qahwa mubarrada
instant coffee	قهوة فورية	qahwa fawriyyah
white coffee	قهوة بحليب	qahwa bi-haliib
coin	عملة معدنية	umla ma'daniyyah
Coke®	Coke®	kook
cold: I have a cold	زكمة: عندي زكمة	zakmah: 'indii zakmah
cold	برودة	buruudah
I'm cold	أنا أشعر بالبرودة	anaa ash'uru bil-buruuda
colour	لون	lawn
comb	مشط	mishtun
to come (arrive)	جاء (وصل)	jaa-a (wasala)
come in!	أدخل!	udkhul!
comfortable	مريح	muriih

English	Arabic	Pronunciation
company (business)	شركة (عمل)	sharika ('amal)
compass	بوصلة	buusala
complaint	الشكوى	ash-shakwaa
computer	حاسوب	haasuub
concert	حفلة موسيقية	hafla muusiiqiyyah
conditioner (for hair)	مكيّف (للشعر)	mukayyif (lish-sha'r)
condoms	الواقيات الجنسية	al-waaqiyaat al-jinsiyyah
conference	مؤتمر	mu-tamar
to confirm	تأكيد	ta-kiid
congratu-lations!	مبروك!	mabruuk!
connection (train, plane)	إتّصال (قطار طائرة)	ittisaal (qitaar, taa-irah)
consulate	قنصلية	qunsuliyyah
British consulate	القنصلية البريطانية	al-qunsuliyyah al-britaaniyyah
American consulate	القنصلية الأمريكية	al-qunsulliyah al-amriikiyyah
contact lens	عدسات لاصقة	adasaat laasiqa
contact lens cleaner	منظف العدسة اللاصقة	munathif al'adasaat al-laasiqa
contraceptives (pill)	موانع الحمل (حبة)	mawaani' al-haml (habbah)
to cook	طبخ	tabakha
cooker	طبّاخ	tabbaakh
to copy (photocopy)	نسخ (ينسخ)	nasakha
copy	نسخة	nuskhah
corkscrew	مفتاح	muftaah
corner	زاوية	zaawiyah
cot	مهد	mahd

English	Arabic	Transliteration
cost: how much does it cost?	يكلف: كم يكلّف؟	yukallif: kam yukallif?
cotton (material)	قطن (مادّة)	qutn (maaddah)
is it cotton?	هل هو قطن؟	hal haathaa qutn?
to cough	يسعل	yas'al
counter	عدّاد	ad-daad
country (not town)	قرية (ليست مدينة)	qaryah (laysat madiinah)
couple (two people)	زوج (شخصان)	zawj (shakhsaan)
crash (collision)	تحطّم	tahaddum
crash helmet	خوذة الأمان	khawthat al-amaan
cream (dairy)	قشطة (معمل ألبان)	qishta (ma'mal albaan)
(cosmetic)	دهن (شكلي)	duhn (shakli)

English	Arabic	Transliteration
credit card	بطاقة الإئتمان	bitaaqatul-i-timaan
crisps	رقائق بطاطس	raqaa-iq al-bataatis
crossroads	تقاطع الطرق	taqaadu' at-turuq
to cry (weep)	بكى (يبكي)	bakaa (yabkii)
cucumber	خيار	khayaar
cul-de-sac	الطريق المسدود	at-tariiq masduud
cup	كأس	ka-s
cupboard	دولاب	duulaab
currant	كشمش	kishmish
current	تيار	tayyaar
cushion	وسادة	wisaada
customs	عادات	aadaat
customs control	الرقابة الجمركية	ar-raqaaba al-jumrukiyya
to cut	قطع	qada'a

cut	قطعة	qit'a
to cycle	يركب الدارجة الهوائية	yarkab adraja al hawai'ya

D

daily	يوميا	yawmiyyan
damage	ضرر	darar
dance	رقص	raqs
to dance	رقص	raqasa
danger	خطر	khatar
dangerous	خطير	khatir
dark	ظلام	thalaam
date (calendar)	تاريخ (تقويم)	taariikh
date of birth	تاريخ الميلاد	taariikh al-miilaad
dates (fruit)	تمر (فاكهة)	tamr (faakiha)
daughter	بنت	bint
dawn	الفجر	al-fajr
day	يوم	yawm
every day	كلّ يوم	kulla yawm
deaf	أصمّ	asam
decaffeinated coffee	قهوة خالية من الكافين	qahwa khaaliya minal kaafiin
December	ديسمبر/كانون الأول	diisamber/ kaanuun al-awwal
deck chair	كرسي المركب	kursiy-yul markab
deep	عميق	amiiq
delay	تأخير	ta-khiir
is there a delay?	هل هناك تأخير؟	hal hunaaka ta-khiir?
delicatessen	دكان لبيع الأطعمة الجاهزة	dukkaan li bay' al-at-'ima al-jaahiza
delicious: this is delicious!	لذيذ: هذا لذيذ!	lathiith: haathaa lathiith!
dentist	طبيب الأسنان	tabiibul-asnaan

dentures أطقم الأسنان atqumul-asnaan
deodorant مزيل الروائح muziel ar-rawaa-ih
department store المخزن الكبير almakhzan al-kabiir
departures مغادرة muqaadarah
deposit إيداع iidaa'
dessert حلوى halwaa
detergent منظّف munathif
diabetic مريض بالسكر mariid bis-sukkar
dialling code رمز الإتصال الهاتفي ramz al-ittisaal al-haatifi
diamond ماس maas
diarrhoea إسهال is-haal
diary مفكرة mufakkira
dictionary قاموس qaamuus
diesel ديزل diizal
diet الحمية (الرجيم) himyah (rijiim)
I'm on a diet أنا أتبع حمية anaa attabi'u himyah
different مختلف mukhtalif
difficult: صعب: هو صعب sas'b: huwa sa'b
it's difficult
dinghy زورق zawraq
dining room غرفة الطعام qurfat at-ta'aam
dinner (evening meal) عشاء (وجبة طعام مسائية) ashaa (wajbat ta'aam masaa-iyyah)
direct flight رحلة مباشر rihla mubaashira
directory (telephone) دليل (هاتف) daliil (haatif)
dirty قذر qathir
disabled (person) معوّق (شخص) mu'awwaq (shakhs)
disco ديسكو disko
discount تخفيض takhfiith

disease	مرض	marath
disinfectant	مطهر	mutahhir
to dive	غاص	qaasa
divorced	مطلّق	mutalliq
I'm divorced	أنا مطلّق	anaa mutalliq
dizzy: I feel dizzy	دوخة: أحس بالدوخة	dawkha: ahissu bid-dawkhka
doctor	طبيب	tabiib
documents	وثائق	wathaa-iq
dog	كلب	kalb
doll	دمية	dumyah
donkey	حمار	himaar
door	باب	baab
double bed	سرير مزدوج	sariir muzdawaj
double room	غرفة ذات سريرين	qurfa thaatu sariirayn
downstairs	الطابق السفلي	at-taabiq as-suflii
dozen	دزينة	daziina
drain	بالوعة	baaluu'a
drawer	درج	daraj
dress	لباس	libaas
to drink	شرب	shariba
drink	شراب	sharaab
drinking water	ماء صالح للشرب	maa saalih lish-shurb
to drive	قاد	qaad
driver	سائق	saa-iq
driving licence	رخصة القيادة	rukhsatul-qiyaada
to drown	غرق	qariqa
drug	مخدّر	mukhaddir
drunk	سكران	sakraan
I'm drunk	أنا سكران	anaa sakraan
dry	جاف	jaaf
dry-cleaner's	التنظيف الجاف	attanthiif al-jaaf
dust	غبار	qubaar

duty-free غير خاضع للضريبة qayr khaa-thi' lith-thariiba

E

ear أذن uthun
early مبكر mubakkir
earrings أقراط (حلق الأذن) aqraat (hilaq al-uthun)
earthquake زلزال zilzaal
east شرق sharq
Easter عيد الفصح iid al-fash
easy سهل sahl
to eat أكل akala
egg بيض bayd
electric كهربائي kahrubaa-ii
electric razor شفرة الحلاقة الكهربائية shafrat al-hilaaqa al-kahrabaa-iyyah
e-mail البريد الإلكتروني al-bariid al-iliktrony
embassy السفارة as-safaara
American embassy السفارة الأمريكية as-safaara al-amriikiyyah
British embassy السفارة البريطانية as-safaara al-britaaniyyah
emergency طوارئ tawaari
empty فارغ faariq
end النهاية an-nihaa-yah
when does it end? متى ينتهي؟ mataa yahtahii?
engaged (to be married) خاطب (لكي يتزوّج) khaatib (likay yatazawwaj)
it's engaged (phone, toilet) هو مشغول (هاتف، مرحاض) huwa mashquul (haatif, mirhaath)
engine محرّك muharrik

England إنجلترا ingeltraa
English (nationality) إنجليزية (جنسية) ingliiziyyah (jinsiyyah)
(language) (لغة) ingliizii
I'm English أنا إنجليزي anaa ingliizii
do you speak English? هل تتكلّم الانجليزية؟ hal tatakallamul-ingliiziyyah?
enjoy: I enjoy swimming تمتّع: أتمتّع بالسباحة tamatu': atamatta'u bissibaaha
enough كاف kaafin
it's not enough غير كاف qayr kaafin
enquiry desk منضدة تحقيق mindadat tahqiiq
to enter دخل dakhala
entertainment ترفيه tarfiih
entrance مدخل madkhal
entrance fee سعر الدخول si'rud-dukhuul
envelope ظرف tharf

escape: fire escape الهروب: سلم النجاة al-huruub: sullam annajaah
Europe أوروبا orobbaa
evening المساء al-masaa
this evening هذا المساء haathal-masaa
tomorrow evening مساء غد masaa-u qad
evening meal وجبة الطعام المسائية wajbat-tud-da'aam
every كلّ kullu
every day كلّ يوم kulla yawm
every year كلّ سنة kulla sanah
everyone كلّ شخص kulla shakhs
excellent ممتاز mumtaaz
excess luggage الأمتعة الإضافية al-amti'a al-ithaafiyyah
exchange تبادل tabaadul
exchange rate سعر الصرف si'rus-sarf

exciting الإثارة al-ithaarah
excuse me! أعذرني! u'thusrnii!
exhibition معرض ma'rad
exit خروج khuruuj
emergency exit مخرج الطوارئ makh-raj at-tawaari
expensive غالي qaali
to expire إنهاء inhaa
to explain توضيح tawdiih
please explain رجاء وضّح rajaa-an waddih
extra إضافي idhaafii
eye عين ayn

F

face الوجه al-wajh
factory المصنع al-masna'
to faint غاب عن الوعي qaaba 'anil-wa'y
to fall سقط saqata
family العائلة al-'aa-ilah
my family عائلتي aa-i-latii
famous مشهور mash-huur
fan المشجع al-mushaj-ji'
far: is it far? بعيد: هل هو بعيد؟ ba'iid: hal huwa ba'iid?
fare (train, bus, etc.) أجرة (قطار، حافلة، الخ) ujrah: (qitaar, haafila, alakh)
farm المزرعة al-mazra'a
farmer المزارع al-muzaari'
fashion الأزياء al-az-yaa
fast الصوم as-sawm
fat (person) سمين (شخص) samiin (shakhs)
(food) دسم (غذاء) dasim (qidaa)
fatty سمين samiin
father الأبّ al-ab
my father أبي abii
fault (defect) عيب (عيب) ayb
favourite مفضّل mufaddal

English	Arabic	Pronunciation
February	فبراير/شباط	fibraayir/shibaat
feel: I feel sick	أشعر: أشعر بالحاجة إلى التقيّا	ash'uru: ash'uru bil-haajati ilaat-taqayyu
I don't feel well	أنا لا أشعر بصحة جيدة	anaa laa ash'uru bi sahhatin jayyida
I feel tired	أشعر بالتعب	ash'uru bitta'ab
ferry	العبّارة	al-'abbaara
few	بضعة	bid'ah
fiancé(e)	خطيب	khatiib
to fill (up)	ملأ	mala-a
fill it up!	إملأه!	im-laa!
film	الفلم	al-film
filter	المرشح	al-murashih
to find	وجد	wajada
fine (to be paid)	غرامة (لكي تدفع)	qaraamah (likay tudfa')
fine (weather)	جميل (طقس)	jamiil (taqs)
finish: when does it finish?	النهاية: متى ينتهي؟	annihaaya: matan-nihaaya?
fire	نار	annaar
fire alarm	جرس الحريق	jarasul-hariiq
fire brigade	الاطفائية	al-itfaa-iyyah
fire exit	مخرج النجاة	makhraj annajaah
fire extinguisher	مطفأة الحريق	mitfa-atul hariiq
fireworks	الألعاب النارية	al-al'aab annaariyyah
first	أول	awwal
the first train	القطار الأول	al-qitaaril-awwal
the first bus	الحافلة الأولى	al-haafila al-uulaa
first aid	الإسعافات الأولية	al-is'aafaat al-awwaliyah

first class الدرجة الأولى ad-darajah al-uulaa
first floor الطابق الأول attaabiq al-awwal
fish سمك samak
to fish صاد saada
fisherman صيّاد السمك sayyaadus-samak
fishing rod سنارة الصيد sannaaratus-sayd
fit: it doesn't fit me ملائم: هو لا يلائمني mulaa-im: huwa laa yulaa-imunii
fix: can you fix it? أصلح: هلّ بالإمكان أن تصلحه؟ aslaha: hal bil imkaani an tuslihahu?
fizzy فوار fawran
flag علم alam
flash (for camera) وميض (لآلة التصوير) wamiid (li-aalat attaswiir)
flask قارورة qaaruurah
flat (apartment) شقّة (شقّة) shuqqah
flat مستو mustawi
flavour نكهة nak-ha
flea برغوث barquuth
flight رحلة rihla
flood فيضان fayadaan
floor أرضية ardiyyah
flour طحين dahiin
flower زهرة zahra
flu إنفلونزا influwanza
fly ذبابة thubaaba
to fly طار taara
fog ضباب dabaab
folder حافظة haafitha
to follow إتّبع ittaba'a
food غذاء qadaa
foot قدم qadam
football (game) كرة قدم (لعبة) kuratul-qadam (lu'bah)

for لـ li
for me لي lii
for sale للبيع lil-bay'
forbidden ممنوع mamnuu'
forecast (weather) توقّع (الطقس) tawaqqu' (attaqs)
foreign أجنبي ajnabi
foreign currency العملة الأجنبية al-'umla al-ajnabiyyah
forest غابة qaabah
forever إلى الأبد ilal-abad
to forget نسى nasaa
fork (for eating) شوكة (لأكل) shawkah (lil-akl)
forward(s) للأمام lil-amaam
fracture الكسر al-kasr
free (unoccupied) شاغر (غير مشغول) shaaqir (qayr mashquul)
(costing nothing) مجانا (لا يكلف شيء) majjaanan (laa yukallifu shay-an)
freezer مجمّدة mujammidah
French فرنسيون firansiyyuun
frequent متكرّر mutakarrir
fresh طازج taazaj
fresh fish سمك طازج samak taazaj
fresh fruit فواكه طازجة faakiha taazijah
fresh milk حليب طازج haliib taazaj
fresh vegetables خضار طازجة khudaar taazijah
Friday جمعة jum'ah
fridge ثلاجة thallaajah
fried (food) مقلي (غذاء) maqlii (qithaa)
friend صديق sadiiq
from من min

front: أمام: الباب الأمامي amaam: al-baab
  front door al-amaamii
frozen مجمّد mujammad
fruit فاكهة faakiha
fruit juice عصير فاكهة asiir faakiha
fruit salad سلطة الفواكه saladatul-faakiha
fuel وقود waquud
full كامل kaamil
full board وجبات كاملة wajabaat kaamila
furniture أثاث athaath
further on أبعد ab'ad
fuse مصهر musahhir
the fuse has blown انفجر المصهر infajara al-musahhir

G

gallery (art) معرض (فنّ) ma'rad (fan)
game (sport) لعبة (رياضة) lu'bah (riyaadah)
(meat) الصيد (لحم) as-sayd (lahm)
garage (private) مرآب (خاصّ) mir-aab (khaas)
(selling petrol, etc.) محطة (بيع بنزين، الخ) mahattah (bay' binziin, alakh)
garden حديقة hadiiqah
garlic ثوم thawm
gas غاز qaaz
gate باب baab
gents toilet مرحاض الرجال mirhaadur-rijaal
genuine أصلي aslii
German (nationality) ألماني (جنسية) almaanii (jinsiyyah)
(language) ألمانية (لغة) almaaniyyah (luqah)
Germany ألمانيا almaaniyaa
to get يصبح yusbihu
to get into دخل dakhala
to get on board ركب rakiba

to get off (bus, etc.) نزل (حافلة، الخ) nazala (haafila)
gift هدية hadiyyah
gift shop دكان الهدايا dukkaan
girl بنت bint
girlfriend صديقة sadiiqa
to give (give back) أعطى (يعيد) a'taa (yu'iidu)
give way إفسح الطريق ifsah at-tariiq
glass (for drink) كأس (للشراب) ka-s (lish-sharaab)
(substance) زجاجة (مادة) zujaajah (maaddah)
a glass of water كأس من الماء ka-s min maa
a glass of wine كأس من النبيذ ka-s minan-nabiid
glasses (spectacles) نظارات nathaaraat
to go ذهب thahaba
to go back عاد aada
to go in دخل dakhala
to go out خرج kharaja
goat عنزة 'anzah
gold ذهب thahaba
golf غولف qolf
golf ball كرة غولف kurat qolf
golf club نادي الغولف naadii al-qolf
golf course ملعب الغولف mal'ab al-qolf
good جيد jayyid
good day يوماً جيداً yawman jayyidan
good evening مساء الخير masaaul-khayr
good morning صباح الخير sabaahul-khayr
goodbye مع السلامة ma'as-salaama
goodnight ليلة سعيدة laylah sa'iidah

grandfather	جدّ	jadd
grandmother	جدة	jaddah
grapefruit	فاكهة الكريب	faakihat al-kreeb
grapefruit juice	عصير فاكهة الكريب	asiir faakihat al-kreeb
grapes	عنب	'inab
greasy: it's too greasy (food)	دهني: هو دهني جدا (غذاء)	duhnii: huwa duhnii jiddan (qithaa)
green	أخضر	akh-tar
greengrocer's	بقال	baqaal
grey	رمادي	ramaadii
grilled	مشوي	mashwii
grocer's	بقال	baqaal
group (of people)	مجموعة (من الناس)	majmuu'ah (minan-naas)
guarantee	ضمان	damaan
guest	ضيف	dayf
guesthouse	دار الضيافة	daarud-diyaafa
guide/ guidebook	دليل/دليل	daliil
guided tour	الجولة الموجّهة	al-jawla al-muwajjaha

H

hair	شعر	sha'r
hair dryer	مجفف الشعر	mujaffifush-sha'r
hairbrush	فرشاة الشعر	furshaarush-sha'r
haircut	حلاقة الشعر	hallaaqush-sha'r
hairdresser	مصفّف الشعر	musaffifush-sha'r
half	نصف	nisf
half an hour	نصف ساّعة	nisf saa'ah
half board	سكن بنصف وجبة	sakan bi nisf wajbah
half bottle	نصف قنينة	nisf qinniinah
ham	لحم الخنزير	laham al-khinziir
hand	يدّ	yad

hand luggage أمتعة يدوية amti'ah yadawiyyah
handbag حقيبة يدوية haqiibah yadawiyyah
handmade صنع يدوي sun' yadawii
to happen حدث hadatha
what happened? ماذا حدث؟ maathaa hadath?
happy سعيد sa'iid
harbour ميناء miinaa
hard (tough) بشدّة (قاسي) bishiddah (qaasii)
hat قبعة qubba'ah
hazelnut بندقة bunduqiyyah
he هو huwa
head رأس ra-s
headache صداع sudaa'
I've got a headache أنا عندي صداع anaa 'indii sudaa'

to hear سمع sami'a
hearing aid مساعدة سمع musaa'idat sam'
heart قلب qalb
heart attack نوبة قلبية nawbah qalbiyyah
heating تدفئة tadfi-ah
heavy ثقيل thaqiil
height إرتفاع irtifaa'
hello مرحبا marhaban
help! ساعدني! saa'idnii!
to help ساعد saa'ada
herbs أعشاب a'shaab
here هنا hunaa
high عالي aalii
high blood pressure ضغط دمّ عالي daqd dam 'aalii
high chair كرسي عالي kursii 'aalii
to hire إستأجر ista-jara

to hitch-hike	إرتحل	irtahala
holiday	عطلة	'utla
home	بيت	bayt
honey	عسل	'asal
honeymoon	شهر العسل	shahrul 'asal
horse	حصان	hisaan
hospital	مستشفى	mustashfaa
hot	حار	haar
it's too hot	هو حار جدا	huwa haar jiddan
hotel	فندق	funduq
hour	ساعة	saa'ah
in an hour's time	خلال ساعة	khilaal saa'ah
house	بيت	bayt
how?	كيف؟	kayfa?
how many?	كم عدد؟	kam 'adad?
how much?	كم؟	kam?
how are you?	كيف أنت؟	kayfa anta?
hungry: I'm hungry	جائع: أنا جائع	jaa-i': anaa jaa-i'
hurry: I'm in a hurry	عجلة: أنا في عجلة	'ajala: anaa fii 'ajala
hurt: it hurts	أذى: إنه يآذي	athaa: innahu yu-aa-thii
husband	زوج	zawj
my husband	زوجي	zawjii

I

I	أنا	anaa
ice	ثلج	thalj
ice-cream	بوظة	bootha
iced coffee	قهوة مبردة	qahwa mubarradah
iced tea	شاي مبرد	shaa-y mubarrad
iced water	ماء مبردة	maa mubarrad
identification	تعريف	ta'riif
ill	مريض	mariid

immediately	فورا	fawran
important	مهم	muhim
included	متضمن	mutadammin
indigestion	عسر الهضم	asrul-hadm
infection	عدوى	'adwaa
information	معلومات	ma'luumaat
information office	مكتب الاستعلامات	matktabul-isti'laamaat
injured	مصاب	musaab
insect	حشرة	ha-sha-rah
insect bite	عضة حشرة	'addatu-hasharah
insect repellent	طارد الحشرات	taaridul-hasharaat
instant coffee	قهوة فورية	qahwa fawriyyah
insurance	تأمين	ta-miin
interesting	مثير	muthiir
international	دولي	duwalii
interpreter	مترجم	mutarjim
to invite	دعى	da'aa
invoice	فاتورة	faatuura
Ireland	إيرلنده	iirlandaa
Irish	آيرلندي	iirlandii
iron (metal)	حديد (معدن)	hadiid (ma'dan)
(for clothes)	كوى (للملابس)	kawaa (lil-malaabis)
island	جزيرة	jaziirah
it	هو/هي	huwa/hiya
itch: it itches	حكّة: يحك	hakka: yahukku

J

jacket	سترة	sutra
leather jacket	سترة جلدية	sutra jildiyyah
jam (food)	مربّى (غذاء)	murabbaa (qithaa)
jammed	مسدود	masduud

January	يناير/كانون الثّاني	yanaayir/ kaanuun ath-thaanii
jar	جرّة	jarrah
jeans	جينز	jiinz
jellyfish	قنديل البحر	qindiilul-bahr
jewellery	مجوهرات	mujawharaat
Jewish	يهودي	yahuudii
I'm Jewish	أنا يهودي	anaa yahuudi
job	وظيفة	wathiifah
joke: it's a joke	نكتة: هذه نكتة	nuktah: haathihii nuktatun
journalist	صحفي	sahafi
journey	رحلة	rihlah
jug	دورق	dawraq
juice	عصير	'asiir
orange juice	عصير البرتقال	'asiirul-burtuqaal
tomato juice	عصير الطماطة	'asiirut-tamaatim
July	يوليو/تموز	yuulyuu/tamuuz
jumper	بلوز	bluuz
junction	تقاطع	taqaatu'
June	يونيو/حزيران	yuunyuu/ huzayraan

K

to keep	احتفظ	ihtafitha
key	مفتاح	miftaah
my key, please	مفتاحي، رجاء	miftaahii, rajaa-an
kind: you're very kind	رحيم: أنت رحيم جدا	rahiim: anta rahiim jiddan
to kiss	قبّل	qabbala
kitchen	مطبخ	matbakh
knee	ركبة	rukbah
knife	سكين	sikkiin
to know	علم	'alima
I know	أنا أعلم	anaa 'alammu
I don't know	أنا لا أعلم	anaa laa 'alammu

L

label (luggage) علامة (أمتعة) 'alaamah (amti'ah)
ladies (toilet) مرحاض السيدات mirhaadus-sayyidaat
lake بحيرة buhayra
lamb حمل hamal
lamp مصباح misbaah
landing هبوط hubuut
late متأخرا muta-akhir
sorry I'm late آسف أنا متأخرا aasif anaa mu-ta-akhir
later لاحقا laahiqan
launderette مغسلة maqsalah
laundry service خدمة المكوجي khidmat al-makwaji
lawyer محامي muhaamii
leather جلد jild
to leave غادر qaadara
left متروك matruuk
left luggage office محل إيداع الحقائب المتروكة mahal iidaa' al-haqaa-ib al-matruuka
leg ساق saaq
lemon ليمون laymuun
lemonade شراب الليمون sharaabul-laymuun
to lend أعار a'aar
to let (allow) سمح (يسمح له) samaha (yasmahu lahu)
licence (driving) رخصة (قيادة سيارة) rukhsa (qiyaadat sayyaarah)
life jacket سترة النجاة sutratun-najaat
lifeboat قارب النجاة qaaribun-najaat
lifeguard حارس الإنقاذ haarisul-inqaad
lift (elevator) مصعد mis'ad

English	Arabic	Pronunciation
light (illumination)	ضوء (إضاءة)	daw (idaa-a)
(lamp)	نور (مصباح)	nuur (misbaah)
(not heavy)	خفيف (ليس ثقيل)	khafiif (laysa thaqiil)
light bulb	مصباح	misbaah
lighter (cigarette)	قداحة (سيجارة)	qaddaaha (sijaara)
to like	أحبّ	ahabba
linen	بطانة	bataana
lipstick	أحمر الشفاه	ahmarush-shifaah
to listen to	إستمع إلى	istama'a ilaa
litter (rubbish)	فضلات (قمامة)	fadalaat (qumaamah)
little (small)	قليلا (صغير)	qalilaalan (saqiir)
to live	عاش	'aasha
to lock	قفل	qafala
lock	قفل	qufl
locker (for luggage)	خزانة (للأمتعة)	khazaanah (lil-amti'a)
long	طويل	tawiil
to look for	بحث عن	bahatha 'an
lorry	الشاحنة	ash-shaa-hina
lost	مفقود	mafquud
lost property office	مكتب الأشياء المفقود	maktabul-ash-yaa al-mafquuda
lot: a lot	كثير	kathiir
lotion	مستحضر	mustah-thir
loud	عالي	'aalii
to love	أحب	ahabba
lovely	رائع	raa-i'
lucky	محظوظ	mah-fuuth
luggage	أمتعة	amti'a
lunch	غداء	qadaa

M

maid	جارية	jaa-riya
main course (of meal)	وجبة رئيسية (من وجبة الطعام)	wajba ra-iisiyyah (min wajbati-ta'aam)
to make	جعل	ja'ala
man	رجل	rajul
manager	المدير	al-mudiir
map	خريطة	khariita
marble	رخام	rukhaam
March	مارس/آذار	maaris/aathaar
marmalade	مربى البرتقال	murabbal-burtuqaal
married	متزوّج	muta-zawwij
match (game)	مباراة (لعبة)	mubaaraa (lu'bah)
matches (light)	كبريت / عود ثقاب (ضوء)	kibriit/'uud thiqaab (daw)
maximum speed	السرعة القصوى	as-sur'a alquswaa
May	مايو/مايس	maayoo/maayis
meal	وجبة الطعام	wajbatu-ta'aam
mean: what does it mean?	المعنى: ماذا يعني هذا؟	al-ma'naa: maathaa ya'nii haathaa?
meat	لحم	lahm
meatball	كرة من اللحم	kurah minal-lahm
medicine	طبّ	tib
to meet	إجتمع	ijtama'a
meeting	إجتماع	ijtimaa'
to mend	أصلح	aslaha
menu	قائمة	qaa-imah
the menu, please	القائمة، رجاء	al-qaa-imah, rajaa-an
message	رسالة	risaalah

English	Arabic	Pronunciation
meter (taxi)	متر (سيارة أجرة)	mitr (sayaaratu ujra)
metre	متر	mitr
microwave (oven)	مايكرويف (فرن)	mikro-weef (furn)
midday	منتصف النهار	muntasafun-nahaar
middle	منتصف	muntasaf
midnight	منتصف الليل	muntasaful-layl
milk	حليب	haliib
mince (meat)	لحم مفروم (لحم)	lahm mafruum (lahm)
mineral water	الماء المعدني	al-maa al-ma'danii
mints	نعناع	ni'naa'
minute	دقيقة	daqiiq
mirror	مرآة	mir-aah
miss (plane, train, etc.)	تغيّب (طائرة، قطار، الخ)	taqayyaba (tayyaarah, qitaar)
missing (thing)	فقدان (شيء)	fuqdaan (shay)
mistake	خطأ	khata
monastery	دير	diir
Monday	الإثنين	al-ithnayn
money	مال	maal
month	شهر	shahr
monument	تمثال	timthaal
moon	قمر	qamar
more	أكثر	akthar
some more...	أكثر ...	akthar...
morning	صباح	sabaah
in the morning	في الصباح	fis-sabaah
tomorrow morning	صباح الغد	sabaahul-qad
this morning	هذا الصباح	hathaas-sabaah

mosque	مسجد	masjid
mosquito net	ناموسية	naamuusiyyah
mosquitoes	بعوض	ba'uutha
mother	الأمّ	al-um
mother-in-law	عمّة	'ammah
motorbike	دراجة نارية	darraajah naariyyah
motorway	الطريق السريع	at-tariiq as-sarii'
mountain	جبل	jabal
mouse	فأر	fa-r
moustache	شارب	shaarib
mouth	فمّ	fam
much	كثير	kathiir
how much?	كم؟	kam?
too much	كثيرا	kathiiran
it's too much (too expensive)	هذا أكثر من المعقول (غالي جدا)	hathaa akthar min ma'quul (qaali jiddan)
museum	متحف	mithaf
music shop	دكان موسيقى	dukkaan muusiiqaa
Muslim	مسلم	muslim
mussels	بلح البحر	balahul-bahr
mustard	خردل	khardal

N

nail (metal)	مسمار (معدن)	mismaar (ma'dan)
(finger, toe)	ظفر (إصبع، إصبع قدم)	thifr
name	الاسم	al-ism
my name is...	اسمي...	ismii...
napkin	المنديل	al-mindiil
nappy	الحفاظة	al-haafitha
narrow	ضيّق	dayyiq
nationality	الجنسية	al-jinsiyyah

English	Arabic	Transliteration
navy blue	الأزرق الداكن	al-azraq ad-daakin
near	قريب	qariib
necessary	ضروري	tharuurii
neck	الرقبة	ar-raqaba
to need	إحتاج	ihtaaja
I need...	أحتاج...	ahtaaju...
I need a car	أحتاج سيارة	ahtaaju sayyaarah
I need to go	أحتاج للذهاب	ahtaaju lith-thahaab
needle	الإبرة	al-ibrah
a needle and thread	إبرة وخيط	ibrah wa khayt
neighbour	الجار	al-jaar
nephew	إبن الأخ	ibnul-akh
never	أبدا	abadan
new	جديد	jadiid
news	الأخبار	al-akhbaar
newspaper	الصحيفة	as-sahiifa
an English newspaper	صحيفة إنجليزية	sahiifa ingiliiziyyah
newsstand	كشك بيع الصحف	kushk bay' as-suhuf
New Year	السنة الجديدة	as-sanah al-jadiidah
New Zealand	نيوزيلندا	niyuu ziilanda
next	التالي	at-taalii
next to	بجانب	bi-jaanib
nice	لطيف	latiif
it's very nice	هو لطيف جدا	huwa latiif jiddan
niece	أبنة الأخت	ibnatul-ukht
night	الليل	al-layl
last night	ليلة أمس	laylata ams
nightclub	النادي الليلي	annaadii al-ahlii
no	لا	laa

English	Arabic	Pronunciation
no, thanks	لا، شكرا	laa, shukrarn
noisy	صاخب	saakhib
non-alcoholic	لا كحولي	laa kuhuulii
a non-alcoholic drink	شراب لا كحولي	sharaab laa kuhuulii
none	لا شيئ	laa shay
there's none left	لم يتبق شيئ	lam yatabaqqa shay
non-smoking	لغير المدخنين	li-qayr al-mudakhiniin
north	الشمال	ash-shamaal
Northern Ireland	آيرلندا الشّمالية	iirlanda ash-shamaaliyyah
nose	الأنف	al-anf
not	ليس	laysa
notebook	دفتر الملاحظات	daftar al-mulaaha-thaat
nothing	لا شيء	laa shay
November	نوفمبر/تشرين الثّاني	nofambar/tishriin ath-thaanii
now	الآن	al-aan
number	العدد	al-'adad
phone number	رقم الهاتف	raqam al-haatif
number plate	رقم السيارة	raqamus-sayyaarah
nurse	الممرضة	al-mumarrithah
nuts (bar nibbles)	بندق (حانة تقضم)	bunduq

O

English	Arabic	Pronunciation
October	أكتوبر/تشرين الأول	oktobar/tishriin al-awwal
octopus	أخطبوط	ukhtubuut
off (radio, engine, etc.)	،منطفىء (راديو محرّك، الخ)	muntafi (raadyo, muharrik)

English	Arabic	Pronunciation
the heating is off	إنّ التدفئة منطفية	innat-tadfi-ata muntafiyah
office	مكتب	maktab
often	في أغلب الأحيان	fii aqlabil-ahyaan
oil	نفط	nift
OK	حسنا	hasanan
old (person)	مسن (شخص)	kabiirus-sin
(thing)	قديم (شيء)	qadiim
how old are you?	كم عمرك؟	kam 'umruka?
I'm ... years old	أنا ... سنوات	anaa ... sanawaat
olive oil	زيت الزيتون	zaytuz-zaytuun
olives	زيتون	zaytuun
on	على	'alaa
once: at once	حالا	haalan
one	واحد	waahid
onion	بصل	basal
only: only one	فقط: واحد فقط	faqad: waahid faqad
open	مفتوح	maftuuh
is it open?	هل هو مفتوح؟	hal huwa maftuuh?
to open	فتح	fataha
opening hours	أوقات الفتح	awqaatul-fath
operator (telephone)	موظف الاتصالات (هاتف)	mu-wath-thaf it-tisaalaat (haatif)
opposite	نظير	nathiir
optician's	فاحص البصر	faahisul-basar
or	أو	aw
orange (colour)	برتقالي (لون)	burtuqaalii (lawn)
orange	برتقال	burtuqaal
orange juice	عصير البرتقال	'asiirul-burtuqaal
orchestra	أوركسترا	orkestira

to order (food)	طلب (غذاء)	talab (qithaa)
other	آخر	aakhar
our	ـنا	naa
out	خارج	khaarij
out: out of order	معطل	mu'attal
oven	فرن	furn
to overtake	إجتاز	ijtaaza
to owe	يدين	yudiinu
owner	مالك	maalik

P

to pack (bags)	حزم (حقائب)	hazama (haqaa-ib)
package tour	رحلة منظّمة	rihla munath-thama
packet	حزمة	hizmah
painful: it's very painful	مؤلم: هو مؤلم جدا	mu-lim: huwa mu-lim jiddan
painkiller	مضاد الآلام	mu-daadul-aalaam
painting (picture)	صورة (صورة)	suurah
pair	زوج	zawj
palace	قصر	qasr
pancake	فطيرة	fatiirah
pants (trousers)	ملابس داخلية (بنطلون)	malaabis daakhiliyyah
paper	ورقة	waraqah
parcel	حزمة	hizmah
parcels counter	مكتب الحزم	marktab al-hizam
pardon!	عفواً!	'afwan!
parents	أباء	aabaa
park	متنزه	muntazah
to park	أوقف	awqafa
part (spare)	قطعة (إحتياطي)	qit'ah (ihtiyaadii)

English	Arabic	Transliteration
partner (business)	شريك (عمل)	shariik ('amal)
my partner (in couple)	شريكي (في الزواج)	shariikii (fiz-zawaaj)
party (celebration)	حفلة (إحتفال)	haflah (ihtifaal)
passenger	مسافر	musaafir
passport	جواز السفر	jawaazus-safar
passport control	جوازات	jawaazaat
pasta	باستا	baastaa
pastry (cake)	معجنات (كعكة)	mu'ajjanaat (ka'kah)
to pay	دفع	dafa'a
peanuts	فستق	fustuq
pearl	لؤلؤة	lu-lu-ah
pedestrian	ماشي	maashii
pedestrian crossing	منطقة عبور المشاة	mantiqat 'ubuur mushaah
pen	قلم	qalam
pencil	قلم الرصاص	qalamur-rasaas
penicillin	بنسلين	binsiliin
pensioner	متقاعد	mutaqaa'id
pepper (spice)	فلفل (تابل)	filfil (taabil)
(vegetables)	فلفل (خضار)	filfil (khuthaar)
per	لكلّ	li-kulli
per hour	بالسّاعة	bis-saa'ah
per kilometre	لكلّ كيلومتر	li-kulli kilomiitar
per week	بالإسبوع	bil-usbuu'
perfect: it's perfect	مثالي: هو مثالي	mithaalii: huwa mithaalii
performance	أداء	adaa
perfume	العطر	al-'itr
person	شخص	shakhs

per person	للشخص الواحد	lish-shakhs al-waahid
petrol	بنزين	binziin
unleaded petrol	البنزين الخالي من الرّصاص	al-binziin al-khaalii minar-rasaas
petrol station	محطة البنزين	mahat-tat al-binziin
phone	هاتف	haatif
phonecard	بطاقة هاتف	bitaaqat haatif
photocopy	إنسخ	insakh
photograph	صورة	suurah
picnic	نزهة	nuzha
picture (on wall)	صورة (على الحائط)	suurah ('alal haa-it)
pie	فطيرة	fatiirah
piece (slice)	قطعة (شريحة)	qit'ah (shariiha)
pier	رصيف	rasiif
pill	حبة	habbah
pillow	وسادة	wisaadah
pin	دبّوس	dabbuus
pink	وردي	wardii
pipe (for smoking)	أنبوب (لتدخين)	unbuub (lit-tadkhiin)
(drain, etc.)	أنبوبة (بالوعة، الخ)	unbuubah (baaluu'ah)
plain	واضح	waadih
plane	طائرة	taa-irah
plaster	لصقة	lasqah
plastic	بلاستيك	balaastiik
plate	صحن	saahn
platform (railway)	رصيف (سكة حديد)	rasiif (sikkat hadiid)
to play	لعب	lu'bah
please	رجاء	rajaa-an

plug (electric) منفذ (كهربائية) manfath (kahrubaa-ii)
(for sink) سدادة (للمغسلة) saddaadah (lil-maqsalah)
plumber سبّاك sabbaak
pocket جيب jayb
poisonous سامّ saam
police شرطة shurtah
police station مركز الشرطة markaz ash-shurtah
polish (for shoes) صقل (للأحذية) saql (lil-ah-thiyah)
pool مسبح masbah
poor (not rich) فقير (ليس غني) faqiir (laysa qani)
pork لحم الخنزير lahmul-khinziir
port (harbour) ميناء (ميناء) miinaa
porter (for door) بواب (للباب) baw-waab
(for luggage) حمال (للأمتعة) habbaal (lil-amti'ah)
possible محتمل muhtamal
to post أرسل arsala
post office مكتب البريد maktabul-bariid
postbox صندوق البريد sunduuqul-bariid
postcard بطاقة بريدية bitaa-qah bariidiyyah
postcode رمز بريدي ramz bariidii
poster ملصق mulsaq
pot (for cooking) قدر (للطبخ) qidr (lit-tabkh)
potato بطاطا bataataa
boiled potatoes بطاطا مغلية bataataa maqliyyah
fried potatoes بطاطا مقلّية bataataa maqliyyah
mashed potato بطاطا مهروسة bataataa mahruusah

English	Arabic	Pronunciation
potato salad	سلطة بطاطا	salatat bataataa
powdered milk	حليب جاف	ħaliib jaaf
prawns	جمبري	jambari
prayers	صلاوات	salaawaat
to prefer	فضل	faddala
I'd prefer tea	أنا أفضّل شاي	anaa ufaddilu shaay
pregnant	حامل	haamil
I'm pregnant	أنا حامل	anaa haamilah
prescription	وصفة	wasfah
present (gift)	هدية (هدية)	hadiyyah
this is a present	هذه هدية	haathihii hadiyyah
pretty	جميل	jamiil
price	سعر	si'r
price list	قائمة الأسعار	qaa-imatul as'aar
private	خاصّ	khaas
private bathroom	حمّام خاصّ	hammaam khaas
probably	محتمل	muhtamal
to pronounce	نطق	nataqa
public holiday	عطلة وطنية	'utla wataniyyah
pudding	حلوى	halwaa
to pull	سحب	sahaba
purple	أرجواني	urguwaanii
to push	دفع	dafa'a
pushchair	كرسي مدفوع	kursii madfuu'
pyjamas	بيجامة	bijaamah

Q

English	Arabic	Pronunciation
quality	جودة	juudah
good quality	جودة عالية	juudah 'aaliyah
poor quality	جودة رديئة	juudah radii-ah
quay	رصيف الميناء	rasiif al-miinaa
queen	ملكة	malikah
question	سؤال	su-aal

English	Arabic	Pronunciation
to queue	أصطف	istaffa
queue	طابور	taabuur
quickly	بسرعة	bi-sur'ah
quiet	هدوء	huduu
quilt	لحاف	lihaaf
R		
rabies	داء الكلب	daa-ul-kalb
race (sport)	ركض (رياضة)	rakatha (riyaathah)
radio	راديو	raadyoo
radish	فجل	fijl
railway	سكة الحديد	sikkat hadiid
railway station	محطة سكة الحديد	mahaddat sikkatul-hadiid
rain	مطر	matar
raincoat	معطف مطر	mi'taf matar
raisins	زبيب	zabiib
rare (steak)	غير مستوي (ستيك)	qayr mustawii
rash (skin)	طفح (جلد)	dafh (jild)
rat	جرذ	jarath
rate: exchange rate	سعر: سعر الصرف	si'r: si'rus-sarf
raw	خام	khaam
razor	شفرة الحلاقة	shafrat al-hilaaqah
to read (book, etc.)	قرأ (كتاب، الخ)	qara-a (kitaab)
ready	جاهز	jaahiz
real	حقيقي/أصلي	haqiiqii/aslii
receipt	إيصال	iisaal
reception (desk)	مكتب الإستقبال	maktabul-istiqbaal
recipe	وصفة	was-fah
to recommend	أوصى	awsaa
red	أحمر	ahmar
red wine	نبيذ أحمر	nabiid ahmar

English	Arabic	Pronunciation
reduction	تخفيض	takhfiid
to refund	نقود مسترجعه	nuquud mustarja'ah
regulations	تعليمات	ta'liimaat
relation (family member)	علاقة (فرد من العائلة)	'ilaaqah (fard min 'aa-ilah)
reliable (person, service)	موثوق (شخص، خدمة)	mawthuuq (shakhs, khidmah)
to remember	تذكر	tathakkara
to rent	إستأجر	ista-jara
rent	إيجار	iijaar
to repair	أصلح	aslaha
to repeat	كرر	karrara
reservation	حجز	hajz
to reserve (room, table, etc.)	حجز (غرفة، منضدة، الخ)	hajaza (qurfah, mindatha)

English	Arabic	Pronunciation
reserved	محجوز	mah-juuz
to rest	إرتاح	irtaaha
restaurant	مطعم	mat'am
retired	متقاعد	mutaqaa-'d
to return	عاد	'aada
return (ticket)	ذهاب و إياب (تذكرة)	thahaab wa iyaab
reverse-charge call	مكالمة بالدفع العكسي	mukaalamah bid-daf' al-'aksii
rice (cooked)	رزّ (مطبوخ)	ruz (matbuukh)
(uncooked)	رزّ (غير مطبوخ)	ruz (qayr matbuukh)
rich (person)	غني (شخص)	qani (shakhs)
(food)	غني (غذاء)	qani (qithaa)
right (correct)	صحيح (صحيح)	sahiih (sahiih
(not left)	(ليس يسار)	laysaa yasaar)
on/to the right	على / إلى اليمين	'alaa/ilaa al-yamiin

ring (for finger)	خاتم (للإصبع)	khaatim (lil-isba')
river	نهر	nahr
road	طريق	tariiq
road map	خارطة	khaaritah
roof	سقف	saqf
room	غرفة	qurfah
room service	خدمة غرفة	khidmat al-qurfah
rope	حبل	habl
rose	وردة	wardah
rotten (food)	متعفّن (غذاء)	muta'affin (qithaa)
route	طريق	tariiq
rowing boat	زورق التجذيف	zawraqut-tajthiif
rubber	مطاط	mattaat
rubbish	قمامة	qumaamah
rucksack	الجربنديّة / حقيبة الظهر	al-jarbindiyyah/ haqiibatuth-thahr
rug	بساط	bisaat

S

sad	حزين	haziin
safe (for valuables)	خزنة	khaznah
safe (medicine, etc.)	سلامة (طبّ الخ.)	salaamah (tib)
sailing	الإبحار	al-ibhaar
sale	بيع	bay'
for sale	للبيع	lil-bay'
salad	سلطة	salatah
salesman	بائع	bii-i'
salmon	سلمون	salamuun
salt	ملح	milh
same	نفسه	nafsuhu
sand	رمل	raml
sandals	صنادل	sanaadil
sanitary towel	المنشفة الصحية	alminshafa as-sihiyyah

sardines	سردين	sirdiin
Saturday	سبت	sabt
sauce	صلصة	salsah
saucepan	قدر	qidr
sausage	سجق	sajq
savoury	الطعام المشهي	at-ta'aam almushahii
to say	قال	qaala
school	مدرسة	nmadrasah
scissors	مقص	miqas
scorpion	عقرب	'aqrab
Scotland	أسكوتلندا	iskotlandaa
Scottish	إسكتلندي	iskotlandii
sculpture	نحت	naht
sea	بحر	bahr
seafood	المأكولات البحرية	al-ma-kuulaat al-bahriyyah
seat (chair); (on bus, train, etc.)	مقعد (كرسي)؛ (على الحافلة، قطار، الخ)	miq'ar (kursi)
reserved seat	مقعد محجوز	miq'ad mahjuuz
seat belt	حزام المقعد	hizaamul-miq'ad
second	الثانية	ath-thaaniyah
second-class	الدرجة الثانية	ad-darajah ath-thaaniyah
a second-class ticket	تذكرة من الدرجة الثانية	that-kara minad-darajah ath-thaaniyah
second-hand	مستعمل	musta'mal
to see	رأى	ra-aa
to sell	باع	baa'a
to send	أرسل	arsala
senior citizen	مسن	musin
separate	منفصل	munfasil
separately	منفصلا	munfasilan
September	سبتمبر/أيلول	sibtamber/ayluul

English	Arabic	Pronunciation
serious	جدّي	jiddii
service	خدمة	khidmah
service charge	رسم الخدمة	rasmul-khidmah
set menu	قائمة مركبة	qaa-imah murakkabah
shade (shadow)	ظلّ (ظلّ)	thalla (thil)
shallow (water)	ضحل (ماء)	dahl (maa)
shampoo	شامبو	shaamboo
to shave	حلق	halaqa
shaver	آلة الحلاقة	aalatul-halq
shaver socket	مقبس آلة حلاقة	miqbasu aalatil-halq
shaving cream	دهن الحلاقة	duhnil-hilaawah
she	هي	hiya
sheep	خراف	khiraaf
sheet (for bed)	غطاء (للسرير)	qitaa (lis-sariir)
shelf	الرفّ	ar-raf
shell	صدفة	sadafah
shellfish	الأسماك الصدفيّة	al-asmaakus-sadafiyyah
ship	سفينة	safiinah
shirt	قميص	qamiis
shoes	أحذية	ah-thiyah
shop	دكان	dukaan
shop assistant	عامل دكان	'aamilud-dukaan
shopping	تسوّق	tasawwuq
short	قصير	qasiir
shorts (short trousers)	شورت (بنطلون قصير)	shoort (bantaloon qasiir)
show	معرض	ma'rad
to show	عرض	'arada
shower (bath)	دش (حمّام)	dush (hammaam)
shrimps	روبيان	ruubiyaan
to shut	أغلق	aqlaqa
shut	مغلق	muqlaq

English	Arabic	Pronunciation
sick: I feel sick	مريض: أشعر بالحاجة إلى التقيّء	mariid: ash'uru bil-haajati ilat-taqayyu
sightseeing	مشاهدة معالم المدينة	mushaahadat ma'aalim al-madiinah
sign (road-, notice, etc.)	لافتة (طريق، ملاحظة، الخ)	laafitah (tariiq, mulaahathah)
to sign (form, cheque, etc.)	وقع (استمارة، صكّ، الخ)	waqqa'a (istimaarah, shiik)
signature	توقيع	tawqii'
silk	حرير	hariir
is it silk?	هل هو حرير؟	hal huwa hariir?
silver	فضة	fiddah
is it silver?	هل هي فضة؟	hal hiya fiddah?
simple (easy); (unadorned)	بسيط (سهل)؛ (غير مزيّن)	basiit (sahl) (qayr muzayyan)

English	Arabic	Pronunciation
single (lone); (ticket); (unmarried)	وحيد	wahiid
I'm single	أنا وحيد	anaa wahiid
single room	غرفة ذات سرير واحد	qurfah thaatu sariir waahid.
sink	مغسلة	maqsalah
sister	أخت	ukht
sit	إجلس	ijlis
size (shoes)	حجم (أحذية)	hajm (ahthiyah)
bigger size	حجم أكبر	hajm akbar
smaller size	حجم أصغر	hajm asqar
skimmed milk	الحليب المقشوط	al-haliib al-muqashat
skin	جلد	jild
skirt	تنورة	tannuurah
sky	سماء	samaa
to sleep	نام	naama

sleeping bag	كيس النوم	kiisun-nawm
sleeping pill	القرص المنومّة	al-qurs al-munawwim
slice	شريحة	shariihah
slippers	نعال	na'aal
slow	بطيئ	batii
small	صغير	saqiir
smaller	أصغر	asqar
to smell	شم	shamma
smell	رائحة	raa-ihah
smile	إبتسامة	ibtisaamah
to smoke	دخن	dakh-khana
smoke	دخان	dukh-khaan
I don't smoke	أنا لا أدخّن	anaa laa udakh-khin
snake	أفعى	af'aa
snorkelling	غوص	qaws
soap	صابون	saabuun
socks	جوارب	jawaarib
socket (electrical)	مقبس (كهربائي)	maqbas (kahrubaa-ii)
soft	ناعم	naa'im
soft drink	مشروب لاكحولي	mashruub laa kuhuulii
sold out	انتهى	intahaa
some	بعض	ba'd
someone	شخص ما	shakhsun maa
something	شيء	shay
sometimes	أحيانا	ahyaanan
son	إبن	ayna
song	أغنية	uqniyah
soon	قريبا	qariiban
sorry: **I'm sorry!**	آسف: أنا آسف!	aasif: anaa aasif!
sort (type)	نوع (نوع)	naw'
soup	شوربة	shoorbah

south جنوب januub
souvenir تحفة tuhfah
souvenir shop دكان التحف dukaan attuhaf
sparkling تألّق ta-alluq
to speak تكلم takallama
do you speak English? هل تتكلّم الانجليزية؟ hal tatakallamul-ingliiziyyah?
I don't speak Arabic أنا لا أتكلّم اللغة العربية anaa laa atkallamul-luqatal 'arabiyyah
special خاصّ khaas
speed سرعة sur'ah
spice تابل taabil
spicy كثير التوابل (حار) kathiir at-tawaabil (haar)
spirits أرواح arwaah
sponge (for cleaning) إسفنج (للتنظيف) isfanj (lit-tanthiif)
spoon ملعقة mil'aqah
sport رياضة riyaadah
spring (season) ربيع (فصل) rabii' (fasl)
square (in town) فناء (في البلدة) fanaa (fil-baldah)
squid سمك الصبّار samakus-sabbaar
stadium ملعب mal'ab
stairs سلم sullam
stamp طابع taabi'
star نجم najm
to start بدأ bada-a
station محطة mahattah
bus station محطة الحافلات mahattatul-haafilaat
train station محطة القطار mahattatul-qitaar
to stay أقام aqaama

still (not fizzy)	ساكن (ليس فوار)	saakin (laysa fawwaar)
to sting (bite); (burn)	لدغ (عضة)	ladaqa ('adda)
wasp sting	لدغة زنبور	ladqat zanbuur
stomach	معدة	ma'idah
stop!	قِف!	qif!
storm	عاصفة	'aasifah
straight on	إلى الأمام	ilaal-amaam
keep straight on	أستمرإلى الأمام	istamir ilal-amaam
street; major thoroughfare	شارع؛ طريق رئيسي	shaari'; tariiq ra-iisii
street map	خريطة الشوارع	khariidat ash-shawaari'
string	خيط	khayt
strong (tea, coffee)	قوي (شاي، قهوة)	qawi (shaay, qahwah)
stuck: it's stuck	إلتصق: هو ملتصق	iltasaqa: huwa multasiq
student	طالب	taalib
stung: I've been stung	لسع: أنا لسعت	lasa'a: anaa lusi'tu
stupid	غبي	qabi
suede	جلد مدبوغ	jild madbuuq
sugar	سكّر	sukkar
suit (clothes)	بدلة (ملابس)	badlah (malaabis)
suitcase	حقيبة	haqiibah
I've lost my suitcase	فقدت حقيبتي	faqat-tu haqiibatii
summer	صيف	sayf
in summer	في الصيف	fis-sayf
sun	شمس	shams
sunbathe	تشمّس	tashammus
sunburn	حرقة الشمس	hurqatush-shams
Sunday	الأحد	al-ahad

sunglasses	نظارات شمسية	nath-thaaraat shamsiyyah
sunshade	شمسيّة / مظلة	shamsiyyah/ mithallah
sunstroke	ضربة الشمس	darbatush-shams
suntan lotion	مستحضر السمرة	mustah-thar as-sumrah
supermarket	السوق المركزي	assuq al-markazii
supplement	ملحق	mulhaq
surfboard	لوح التزلج	lawh attazalluj
surfing	تزلج	tazalluj
surname	لقب	allaqab
sweater	بلوز	bluuz
sweet	حلوى	halwaa
sweetener	محلّي	muhallii
sweets	حلويات	halawiyyaat
to swim	سبح	sabaha
swimming pool	مسبح	masbah
is there a swimming pool?	هل هناك مسبح؟	hal hunaaka masbah?
swimsuit	كسوة السباحة	kiswat as-sibaaha
switch	مفتاح	miftaah
to switch on	شغل	shaqqala
to switch off	أطفأ	atfa-a
swollen (finger, ankle, etc.)	إنتفخ (إصبع، كاحل، الخ)	intafakha (isba', kaahil)

T

table	طاولة	taawilah
table tennis	كرة الطاولة	kuratud-daawilah
to take	أخذ	akhatha
can I take pictures?	هلّ مسموح أن أصور؟	hal masmuuh an usawwir?

will you take a picture of us?	ممكن تلتقط صورة منّا؟	mumkin taltaqid suurah minnaa?
to talk	تكلم	takallama
tall	طويل	tawiil
tap	صنبور	sunbuur
tape (cassette)	شريط (كاسيت)	shariit (kaseet)
taste: can I taste some?	ذوق: هلّ بالإمكان أن أتذوق هذا؟	thawq: hal bil-imkaani an atathawwaqa haathaa?
tasty	لذيذ	lathiith
tax	ضريبة	thariibah
taxi	سيارة الأجرة	sayyaaratul-ujrah
tea	شاي	shaay
teabag	كيس الشاي	kiisush-shaay
teacher	معلّم	mu'allim
team (football, etc.)	فريق (كرة قدم، الخ)	fariiq (kurat qadam)
teeth	أسنان	asnaan
telephone	هاتف	haatif
to telephone	اتصل	ittasala
can I telephone from here?	هلّ بالإمكان أن اتصل من هنا؟	hal bil-imkaani an attasila min hinaa?
telephone box	الهاتف العام	al-haatif al-'aam
telephone call	مكالمة هاتفية	makaalamah haatifiyyah
international call	مكالمة دولي	makaalamah duwaliyyah
telephone directory	دليل التلفونات	dalilut-tilifoonaat
television	تلفزيون	tilifizyoon
temperature (fever)	درجة الحرارة؛ (حمّى)	darajatul-haraarah (hummaa)

I have a temperature	عندي ارتفاع في درجة الحرارة	'indll irtifaa' fii darajat al-haraarah
what is the temperature?	ما درجة الحرارة؟	maa darajatul-haraarah?
temporary	مؤقت	mu-aqqat
tennis	تنس	tenis
I'd like to play tennis	أنا أودّ أن ألعب التنس	anaa awaddu an al'abat-tenis
do you play tennis?	هل تلعب التنس؟	hal tal'abut-tenis?
tennis ball	كرة تنس	kuratut-tenis
tennis court	ملعب التنس	mal'abut-tenis
tennis racket	مضرب تنس	midrabut-tenis
tent	خيمة	khaymah
terrace	شرفة	shurfah
tetanus	داء الكزاز	daa-ul-kazzaaz
thank you	شكرا لكم	shaukran lakum
thanks	شكرا	shukran
that	ذلك	thaalika
theatre	مسرح	masrah
there: there is.../there are...	هناك: هناك... / هناك ...	hunaak: hunaaka... / hunaaka...
is there...?	هل هناك... ؟	hal hunaaka...?
these	هؤلاء	haa-ulaa
they	هم	hum
thief	لصّ	lis
thin	رقيق	raqiiq
to think	أعتقد	a'taqidu
I think so	أعتقد ذلك	a'taqidu thaalika
I don't think so	أنا لا أعتقد ذلك	anaa laa a'taqidu thaalika
thirsty: I'm thirsty	عطشان: أنا عطشان	'atshaan: anaa 'atshaan
this	هذا	haathaa

English	Arabic	Pronunciation
those	أولئك	ulaa-ika
thread	خيط	khayt
Thursday	الخميس	al-khamiis
ticket	تذكرة	tathkarah
single ticket	تذكرة ذهاب فقط	tathkarat thahaab faqat
return ticket	تذكرة ذهاب واياب	tathkarat thahaab wa iyaab
ticket office	مكتب التذاكر	maktabut-tathaakir
tie	ربطة العنق	rabdat al-'unuq
tight: it's too tight	ضيّق: هو ضيّق جدا	dayyiq: huwa dayyiq jiddan
tights	جوارب	jawaarib
time	وقت	waqt
timetable	جدول المواعيد	jadwal al-mawaa'iid
tin opener	مفتاح العلب	miftaah al-'ilab
tip (to waiter, etc.)	بقشيش (إلى النادل، الخ)	baqshiish (ilan-naadil)
tired	متعب	mut'ab
tissues	أنسجة	ansigah
to see GRAMMAR	الى	ilaa
to the station	إلى المحطة	ilal-mahaddah
toast	خبز محمص	khubz muhamas
tobacconist's	بائع السجائر	baa-i' as-sajaa-ir
today	اليوم	al-yawm
together	سوية	sawiyyatan
toilet	مرحاض	mirhaad
toilet paper	ورق المرحاض	waraqul-mirhaad
there is no toilet paper	ليس هناك ورق مرحاض	laysa hunaaka waraq mirhaad
token	نقود	nuquud
toll (on motorway, etc.)	ضريبة (على الطريق السريع، الخ)	thariibah ('alat-tariiq as-saarii')

tomato طماطم tamaatlm
tomato juice عضير الطماطم 'asiirut-tamaatim
tomato salad سلطة طماطم saltat tamaatim
tomorrow غدا qadan
tomorrow morning صباح الغد sabaahal-qad
tomorrow evening مساء غد masaa-al-qad
tonight اللّيلة allaylah
tooth سنّ sin
toothache وجع الأسنان waja'ul-asnaan
toothbrush فرشاة الأسنان furshaatul-asnaan
toothpaste معجون الأسنان ma'juunul-asnaan
torch (electric) مصباح (كهربائي) misbaah (kahrubaa-ii)
total مجموع majmuu'
tough (meat) غير ناضج (لحم) qayr nadij (lahm)
tour جولة jawlah
tourist سائح saa-ih
tourist office مكتب السياحة maktabus-siyaahah
towel منشفة minshafah
tower برج burj
town بلدة baldah
town hall دار البلدية daarul-baladiyyah
toy لعبة lu'bah
traditional تقليدي taqliidii
traffic مرور muruur
traffic lights إشارات المرور ishaaratul-muruur
train قطار qitaar
trainers (shoes) أحذية جري (أحذية) ah-thiyat jari
to translate ترجم tarjama
to travel سافر saafara

travel agent وكيل السفريات wakiilus-safariyyaat
traveller's cheques صكوك المسافرين sukuukul-musaafiriin
tree شجرة shajarah
trip: a day trip رحلة: رحلة نهارية rihlah: rihla nahaariyyah
trousers بنطلون bantaloon
trout تراوت trawt
truck شاحنة shaahinah
true: *that's true* حقيقة: هذه حقيقة haqiiqah: haathihiil-haqiiqah
that's not true هذه ليست حقيقة haathihii laysat haqiiqah
trunks (swimming) بنطلون سباحة (سباحة) bantaloon sibaahah (sibaahah)
try on: can I try it on? جرب: هلّ بالإمكان أن أجربه علي؟ jarraba: hal bil-imkaani an ujarribahu 'alay?
t-shirt فانيلة faanillah
Tuesday الثّلاثاء ath-thulaa
tuna سمك التونا samakut-tuunah
tunnel نفق nafaq
turkey الديك الرومي addiikur-ruumii
Turkish bath الحمّام التركي al-hammaam at-turki
to turn off (radio, light) أطفأ (راديو، ضوء) atfa-a (raadyoo, daw)
to turn on فتح fataha
tweezers ملقط milqad
twins توأم taw-am

U

ugly قبيح qabiih
umbrella شمسية shamsiyyah

uncomfortable	مزعج	muz'ij
to understand	فهم	fahima
I don't understand	أنا لا أفهم	anaa laa afham
do you understand?	هل تفهم؟	hal tafham?
underwear	ملابس داخلية	malaabis daakhiliyyah
unemployed	عاطل	'aatil
university	جامعة	jaami'ah
unleaded petrol	البنزين الخالي من الرّصاص	al-binziin al-khaali minar-rasaas
unlucky	سيئ الحظ	say-yi-ul hath
upstairs	الطابق العلوي	at-taabiq al-'ulwii
urgent: it's urgent	مستعجل: هذا مستعجل	musta'jil: haathaa musta'jjil
to use	إستعمل	ista'mala
useful	مفيد	mufiid
usually	عادة	haadatan

V

vacancy (room)	شاغر (غرفة)	shaaqir (qurfah)
valid	صحيح	sahiih
valuables	الأشياء الثمينة	al-ashyaa ath-thamiinah
van	شاحنة	shaa-hinah
VAT	ضريبة	thariibah
veal	لحم العجل	lahmul-'ijl
vegetable	خضار	khuthaar
vegetarian	نباتي	nabaatii
very	جدا	jiddan
very good	جيد جدا	jayyid jiddan
view	منظر	manthar
village	قرية	qaryah
vineyard	مزرعة العنب	mazra'atul-'inab

visa	تأشيرة	ta-shiirah
to visit	زار	zaara
visitor	زائر	zaa-ir

W

to wait (for)	إنتظر (على)	intathara
please wait	الرجاء الإنتظار	ar-rajaa al-intithaar
waiter/ waitress	نادل/نادلة	naadil/naadilah
waiting room	غرفة الإنتظار	qurfatul-intithaar
to wake up	إستيقظ	istayqatha
Wales	ويلز	wiilz
to walk	مشى	mashaa
walk (activity); (route)	مشي (نشاط)؛ (طريق)	mashaa (nashaat); (tariiq)
walking stick	عكازة	'ukkaazah
wallet	محفظة	mahfathah
to want	أراد	araada
war	حرب	harb
wardrobe	خزانة	khizaanah
warm	دافئ	daafi
to wash	غسل	qasala
washbasin	حوض الغسيل	hawth al-qasiil
washing machine	غسّالة	qassaalah
washing powder	مسحوق الغسيل	mashuuqul-qasiil
wasp	زنبور	zanbuur
watch (wrist)	ساعة (رسغ)	sahaat (risq)
water	ماء	maa
mineral water	ماء معدني	maa ma'dani
fresh water	ماء عذب	maa 'athb
waterfall	شلال	shallaal
waterproof	معطف	mi'taf
water-skiing	التزحلق على الماء	attazahluq 'alaal-maa

wave موجة mawjah
way: Is this the right way? الطريق: هل هذا هو الطريق الصحيح؟ attariiq: hal haathaa huwat-tariiq?
way out مخرج makhhraj
we نحن naĥnu
weak (tea, coffee, drink, etc.) خفيف (شاي، قهوة، شراب) khafiif (shaay, qahwah, sharaab)
to wear لبس labisa
weather forecast توقّعات حالة الطقس tawaqqu'aat haalatut-taqs
wedding زفاف zafaaf
wedding ring خاتم الزواج khaatamuz-zawaaj
Wednesday الأربعاء al-arbi'aa
week إسبوع isbuu'
last week الأسبوع الماضي al-isbuu' al-maathii
next week الإسبوع القادم al-isbuu' al-qaadim
weekend عطلة نهاية الإسبوع 'utlat nihaayat al-usbuu'
weekly إسبوعي isbuu'ii
weight وزن wazn
welcome! مرحبا! marhabaa!
well حسنا hasanan
well done (meat) مطهي جيدا (لحم) hathii jayyidan (lahm)
west غرب qarb
wet مبلول mabluul
wetsuit ملابس الغوص malaabis al-qaws
what ما maa
what is it? ما هو؟ maa haathaa?

wheelchair كرسي المعوّقين kursiyyul-mu'awwaqiin
when? متى؟ mataa?
where? أين؟ atna?
which? أيّ؟ ayyu?
which one? أيّ واحد؟ ayyu waahid?
white أبيض abyad
who من man
whole كلّ kulli
whose: لمن: لمن هذا؟ liman: liman haathaa?
whose is it?
why لماذا limaathaa
wife زوجة zawjah
window (house); (shop) نافذة (بيت)؛ (دكان) naafithah (bayt); (dukkaan)
windsurfing ركوب الرياح rukuubur-riyaah
windy: عاصف: الجو 'aasif: al-jawwu
it's windy عاصف 'aasif
wine نبيذ nabiid
red wine النبيذ الأحمر annabiid al-ahmar
white wine النبيذ الأبيض annabiid al-abyad
wine list قائمة النبيذ qaa-imat annabiid
the wine list, please قائمة النبيذ، رجاء qaa-imat annabiid, rajaa-an
winter شتاء shitaa
with مع ma'a
without بدون bidoon
woman إمرأة imra-ah
wood (substance) خشب (مادة) khashab (maaddah)
word كلمة kalimah
to work عمل 'amila

it doesn't work	هو لا يعمل	huwa laa ya'mal
to write	كتب	kataba
writing paper	ورق الكتابة	waraqul-litaabah
wrong	خاطئ	khaati

X

x-ray	الاشعة السينية	al-ashi'ah assiiniyyah

Y

yacht	مركب	mirkab
year	سنة	sanah
this year	هذه السنة	haathihis-sanah
yellow	أصفر	asfar
yes	نعم	na'am
yesterday	أمس	ams
you	أنت	anta
youth hostel	فندق الشباب	funduq ash-shabaab

Z

zero	صفر	sifr
zip	الرمز البريدي	arramz al-bariidii
zoo	حديقة الحيوانات	hadiiqatul-hayawaanaat

Further titles in Collins' phrasebook range
Collins Gem Phrasebook

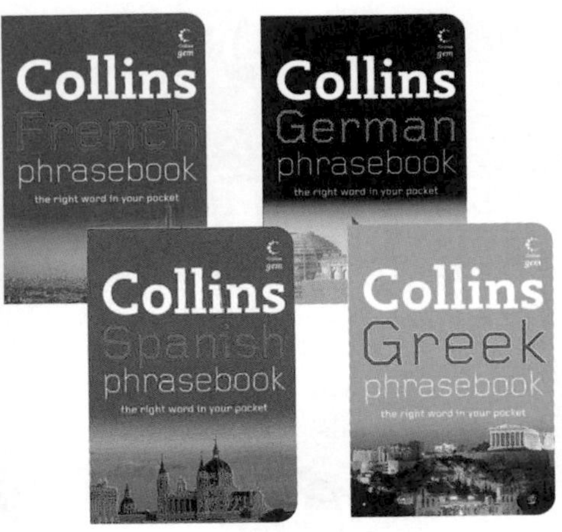

Also available as **Phrasebook CD Pack**

Other titles in the series

Arabic	Greek	Polish
Cantonese	Italian	Portuguese
Croatian	Japanese	Russian
Czech	Korean	Spanish
Dutch	Latin American Spanish	Thai
French	Mandarin	Turkish
German		Vietnamese